Within the pages of every book lies a runway of i stylish harmony. Reading is the ultimate fashion in the finest fabrics of knowledge and creativity. Explore the beauty of Fashion Facts, where every page unfolds a new trend in the art of elegance.

Sarita Hafit

Our Trivia Books

INTRODUCTION

Welcome to **Fashion History Facts**, Theis Ultimate Fashion and Beauty Accessories Trivia, is your comprehensive guide to the captivating world of fashion and beauty. It's a treasure trove of knowledge, featuring 650 multiple-choice questions covering every aspect of fashion history, clothes, footwear, hairstyles, jewelry, fashion models, designers, and much more. Delve into the fascinating journey of the fashion world and the people who shaped it, from iconic designers to trailblazing models and visionary stylists. Explore the evolution of fashion through the ages, from the extravagant styles of the 80s to the timeless elegance of the 70s. Uncover intriguing facts about the history of shoes, hair trends, iconic fashion moments, and the ever-changing landscape of beauty.

Whether you're a fashion enthusiast, a trivia aficionado, or simply curious about the world of style, this book offers something for everyone. From the origins of fashion design to the rise of fashion icons, each page is filled with insights and anecdotes that will deepen your appreciation for this dynamic industry.

Dive into the pages of fashion and let every stitch tell a story. Explore the runway of imagination with the elegance of words. So, grab your favorite accessory, sit back, and prepare to embark on a journey through the captivating world of fashion and beauty. Let the game begin!

CONTENT

CLOTHES FUN FACTS

Zip-a-dee-doo-dah Trivia

1. **What invention is Elias Howe better recognized for, despite patenting an 'Automatic, Continuous Clothing Closure' in 1851 that he didn't pursue further?**
   a. Sewing machine
   b. Vacuum cleaner
   c. Dishwasher
   d. Buttons

2. **What did Whitcomb Judson introduce at the 1893 World's Fair as his 'Clasp Locker,' which failed to impress the world?**
   a. Gloves
   b. Luggage
   c. Shoes
   d. Diving suit

3. **Who was the Universal Fastener Company employee who obtained a patent in 1917 for a device known as the Separable Fastener, which we now recognize as the modern zipper?**
   a. Gideon Sundback
   b. Alexander Graham Bell
   c. Thomas Edison
   d. Benjamin Franklin

4. **What type of product was the first to incorporate a zipper when the B. F. Goodrich Company utilized the Separable Fastener, renaming it "zipper," for this new item?**
   a. Dresses
   b. Rubber boots
   c. Trousers
   d. Sleeping bags

5. **In the 1930s, when the zipper gained widespread use in clothing, which market initially embraced it?**

a. Pets' accessories
b. Men's clothing
c. Children's clothing
d. Women's clothing

6. **What catchy name was coined by zipper manufacturers during their campaign to persuade consumers of the necessity for a new type of fastener in the expanding clothing market?**

a. Openitis
b. Closure
c. Shuttism
d. Gaposis

7. **Which aspect of clothing removal and quick replacement was highlighted in the initial marketing of zippers for clothing, emphasizing the convenience factor, with a nod to the suggestive undertones that "sex sells"?**

a. Men's trousers
b. Neither of these
c. Women's dresses
d. Both of these

8. **True or False: Airtight and watertight zippers used for space suits and hazmat suits use a mechanism similar to the closure of a plastic ziploc bag.**

a. True
b. False

9. **What was the name of the leading Japanese zipper manufacturer at the beginning of the 21st century?**

a. YKK
b. ZIP
c. UPS
d. HIT

10. **Which of the following modern advancements in fastening mechanisms has been employed to substitute zippers in certain applications?**
a. Buckles
b. Velcro
c. Buttons
d. Laces

Don't Remove Your Kilt!

11. **What garment is typically worn beneath a kilt in traditional Scottish attire?**
a. A second, smaller kilt
b. Nothing
c. A brace
d. Leather

12. **Which Roman garment, known for its simplicity as it's often just a cloth draped around the body, remains popular at parties despite being past its prime?**
a. Poncho
b. Toga
c. Culottes
d. Chiton

13. **During the seventeenth century, which group commonly wore dark dresses with ankle-length and full sleeves?**
a. The Moors
b. The Scientologists
c. The Puritans
d. The Slaves

14. **Which risqué swimwear, named after the site of a nuclear bomb test, gained popularity after being modeled by a Parisian nude dancer?**
a. Bikini

b. Monokini
c. Tankini
d. Speedo

15. Whose conical bra, worn during her 'Blonde Ambition' tour, became an infamous fashion choice for its sexual implications?

a. Britney Spears
b. Joan Jett
c. Janet Jackson
d. Madonna

16. What trends in women's fashion during the early 2000s commonly resulted in the exposure of what, typically peering over the waistbands of low-rise jeans?

a. Chastity belts
b. Hemp belts
c. Men's boxer shorts
d. G-strings

17. What defining feature was notable about Jennifer Lopez's sheer, green Versace dress, famously worn at the Grammy Awards in 2000?

a. It was crafted with transparent fabric
b. It had a deep, plunging neckline
c. It was adorned with more than fifty pounds of jewels
d. It was form-fitting and vacuum-sealed

18. In which movie did the Mankini gain prominence as a novelty swimwear piece for men during the 2000s?

a. Eyes Wide Shut
b. EuroTrip
c. Borat
d. Animal House

19. What fashion accessory is employed in tightlacing, the practice of constraining the body's natural shape?

a. Choker necklace
b. Sneakers
c. Corset
d. Foot bindings

20. **What material was Lady Gaga's dress entirely composed of when she accepted the Video of the Year award at the 2010 MTV Video Music Awards?**
a.   Live birds
b.   Stained glass
c.   Saran wrap
d.   Raw flank steak

Beyond the Little Black Dress

21. **Which renowned fashion designer is attributed with popularizing the Little Black Dress (LBD)?**
a.   Christian Dior
b.   Calvin Klein
c.   Gianni Versace
d.   Gabrielle ("Coco") Chanel

22. **In fashion guides for women, a sweater or sweater set is often recommended as a staple. What natural fiber is considered the most desirable for crafting these garments?**
a.   silk
b.   linen
c.   cashmere
d.   Nylon

23. **Which iconic Hollywood actress notably incorporated pants into her personal style, setting a trend for women in the modern era, despite the garment's initial association with men's attire?**
a.   Katharine Hepburn
b.   Audrey Hepburn
c.   Elizabeth Taylor
d.   Grace Kelly

24. Among the plethora of coveted shoe styles, high heels, spikes, and stilettos stand out as favorites among women for their leg-lengthening allure. Leading this trend towards increasingly towering heels is a renowned French shoe designer celebrated for his signature "sammy red-bottoms." Who is this prominent figure in the world of fashion footwear?

a. Jimmy Choo
b. Bruno Magli
c. Manolo Blahnik
d. Christian Louboutin

25. Moving on to outerwear: Fashion experts concur that the trench coat stands as the epitome of versatility. Suited for various climates and occasions, from casual to formal settings, it remains a timeless wardrobe staple. Which renowned English company, with roots dating back to World War I, is famed for crafting a distinctive iteration of the trench coat that continues to be sought after worldwide?

a. Fortnum and Mason
b. Marks and Spencer
c. Harrod's
d. Burberry

26. While the Little Black Dress holds a special place in many women's hearts, there are occasions that call for a more versatile option. Enter the iconic jersey wrap dress, a staple in modern women's wardrobes since the 1970s, seamlessly transitioning from work attire to evening dinners or church gatherings. Who is the innovative designer behind this timeless fashion classic?

a. Diana Vreeland
b. Grace Mirabella
c. Anna Wintour
d. Diane von Furstenberg

27. For every fashionista fixated on shoes, there's another enamored with handbags. Women cherish their bags, whether it's a purse, clutch, satchel, or tote, considering them indispensable accessories for their busy lifestyles. At the

zenith of handbag fashion stands a style crafted by Hermes, bearing the name of a British actress who found fame as an expatriate in France. What is this iconic handbag style?

a. Birkin bag
b. Scott Thomas bag
c. Mirren bag
d. Rampling bag

28. While defining a single jewelry piece as a wardrobe essential is challenging, many consider the pearl necklace a timeless staple. Evolving in lengths, sizes, shapes, and hues over the years, pearl necklaces have maintained their allure. Few have embraced this trend as gracefully as two distinct US First Ladies, both celebrated for their elegant pearls despite their differing backgrounds. Who are these iconic pairs of First Ladies?

a. Eleanor Roosevelt and Nancy Reagan
b. Lady Bird Johnson and Betty Ford
c. Mamie Eisenhower and Michelle Obama
d. Jacqueline Kennedy and Barbara Bush

29. Denim jeans reign as one of the most prevalent clothing items globally, transcending mere utility to become a fashion staple. Available in a myriad of styles, from stonewashed to distressed, skinny to wide-leg, denim jeans cater to diverse tastes and preferences. Yet, amidst their ubiquity, one question remains: Who is credited with inventing the iconic "blue jeans"?

a. An Unknown Wrangler
b. Robert E. Lee
c. Gloria Vanderbilt
d. Jacob Davis and Levi Strauss

30. Continuing our exploration of iconic dresses, let's delve into the realm of wedding attire with the "WWD" or White Wedding Dress. Legend has it that a particular individual sparked the tradition of brides donning white gowns on their special day. Who is credited with igniting this timeless fashion trend?

a. Marie Antoinette
b. Queen Victoria of England
c. Scarlet O'Hara
d. Guinevere

Styles of Swimwear

31. Derived from the former name for a swimming pool, what was the traditional term used for a one-piece swimming costume?
a. Dip suit
b. Dive suit
c. Swimming hole suit
d. Tank suit

32. Which influential religious institution condemned the bikini as sinful upon its introduction in 1946?
a. Chief Rabbi in Israel
b. The Mormon Church
c. The Vatican
d. General Synod of the Anglican Church

33. Male boardshorts were originally known by what name?
a. Wavers
b. Fish and dips
c. Divers
d. Surf Trunks

34. Created in 1995, which bikini style, considered highly inappropriate and bordering on indecent, challenges the boundaries of decency and might as well be avoided altogether?
a. Atomkini
b. Microkini
c. Pulsarini
d. Protonkini

35. What element is absent in a monokini?
a. The sides
b. The top

c. The bottom

d. The front

36. **What is the term commonly used to refer to the swimwear typically worn by men in competitive team sports?**

a. Trunks

b. Togs

c. Manline

37. **The bandeaukini is another favored swimwear choice among women. What distinctive feature is notably absent in this style?**

a. Bared midriff

b. Backs

c. Shoulder straps

d. Bottoms

38. **In an era where bikinis are increasingly minimal and revealing, the tankini stands out as an exception, gaining popularity among women. What sets this fashion trend apart?**

a. It features a type of crop top

b. It features a top worn back to front

c. It features ankle length pants

d. It features a polo neck collar

39. **The jammer, gaining popularity among male competitive athletes, bears a resemblance to what type of garment?**

a. Pyjamas

b. An upside down umbrella

c. A caftan

d. Cycling shorts

40. **Despite the often strict dress codes for women within certain faiths, what is the term used to describe the swimwear permitted for some Muslim women?**

a. Burquini

b. Hijabini

c. Khimarnini

d. Niqabini

Chest of Drawers

41. Today known as panties, in my grandmother's era, these undergarments were commonly referred to by another name. What was it?

a. Bagalettes
b. Bloopers
c. Bloomers
d. Bagpants

42. Before the 1960s, modesty standards for women differed significantly from today's norms. How did women of your grandmother's generation typically manage their figure?

a. Corsage
b. Corset
c. Corvair
d. Coupe

43. Despite the prevalence of thick, worsted skirts worn year-round by your grandmother, she invariably donned one of these "unmentionables" underneath. What undergarment was it?

a. Underlayer
b. Pattyskirt
c. Petitpoint
d. Petticoat

44. Today we wear sexy camisoles with or without blouses and bras, but in my grandmother's day they were functional garments known by which name?

a. Underblouse

b. Bolero

c. Bodice

d. Buster

45. During your grandmother's youth, attaining an 18-inch waist was considered essential. What garment did she wear to achieve this remarkable feat?

a. Waist whittler

b. Waist waster

c. 18-incher

d. Throttler

46. Pantyhose and fake tan have rendered these essential items obsolete in your grandmother's dresser. What were these staple garments?

a. Stockings

b. Thongs

c. Socks

d. Slippers

47. In your grandmother's era, there were two types of "unmentionable" belts. One was a sanitary belt designed to secure a pad in place. What was the name of the other type of belt?

a. Chastity belt

b. Waister belt

c. Leg belt

d. Suspender belt

48. My grandmother used the French name for this "unmentionable," a term that persists in its abbreviated form today. In German, however, what was the name for it, which better reflects its function?

a. Bustenhalter

b. Titzling

c. Bustenzling

d. Titzenhalter

49. **Among the most discreet items in your grandmother's dresser were those she ceased using at menopause. What were these items?**
a. Condoms
b. Handmade washable fabric sanitary pads
c. Maternity smocks
d. Chastity belts

50. **Actually, your grandmother didn't have one of these in her dresser because her derriere was ample enough, and it symbolized a fashion trend that predates her era. What was it?**
a. Bumbag
b. Buttocker
c. Booty Enhancer
d. Bustle

It Was the Vest of Times

51. **In a three-piece suit, comprising trousers/pants and a jacket/overcoat, the final component, worn beneath the jacket/overcoat, is termed a vest in the US and Canada. What is this piece called in Britain and numerous other countries?**
a. Hipjacket
b. Belly Button-up
c. Thighsweater
d. Waistcoat

52. **A T-shirt or sleeveless top, typically white and worn beneath clothing, is referred to as a vest in the United Kingdom and an undershirt in the US and Canada. What is this garment commonly called in Australia and Asia?**
a. Onesy
b. Singlet
c. Firster

d. Onlywear

53. **These sleeveless garments, alternatively known as pullovers or tank tops, are typically worn over a T-shirt or dress shirt. Available in various colors such as black, brown, gray, and featuring diverse patterns like argyle, they commonly have a V neckline. What are these vests called?**
a. Sweater vest
b. Tank-vest
c. No-armed vest
d. Vestibule

54. **This attire is referred to as a vest in Indian English and an undershirt in American English. However, it also shares historical roots as a garment worn in the 18th century, showcasing influences from Persian and Asian cultures. What garment does this description suggest?**
a. Cassock
b. Sari
c. Banyan
d. Kimono

55. **This protective garment, originally devised by a woman, serves as vital gear for police officers, shielding their chest from potential gunfire. What type of vest is this?**
a. Chain-mail vest
b. Bullet-proof vest
c. Heart-safe vest
d. Chest-shield vest

56. **This type of vest is frequently donned by bikers and punks alike, earning various monikers such as a battle jacket within the extreme metal community. What specific type of vest does this describe?**
a. Kutte
b. Wutte
c. Butte
d. Mutte

57. This snug-fitting, typically sleeveless men's jacket is predominantly crafted from light-colored leather. Throughout the 16th and 17th centuries, it was frequently worn atop a doublet. What is this garment, sometimes characterized as "rude," called?
a. Dorkin
b. Nerdin
c. Jerkin
d. Geekin

58. Which type of vest is commonly matched with a hat embellished with jigs or plugs, sturdy trousers, and boots, often accompanied by galoshes? This vest typically features numerous pockets designed to hold additional tackle.
a. Football vest
b. Soccer vest
c. Bowling vest
d. Fishing vest

59. Crafted from looped yarn of the same name, this vest prioritizes warmth over style. Its exterior is looped while the interior remains smooth, ensuring optimal insulation for the wearer. This type of yarn is also frequently employed in rug making. What is this vest called?
a. Bouclé
b. Ribbon
c. Flammé
d. Eyelash

60. The term "vest" originates from the Italian word "veste" or "vesta," which, when translated, literally means what?
a. Coat
b. Robe
c. Sleeveless
d. Warmth

My Rented Tux Trivia

61. What is the origin of the term "tuxedo"?
a. It was the name of the first tailor to make the suit.
b. It is slang from "luxury doings".
c. It is the Italian word for dinner jacket.
d. It is the name of a town and country club.

62. What material might the very shiny shoes that accompanied my rental tuxedo have been made of, eliminating the need for polishing?

a. suede
b. nylon
c. patent leather
d. Canvas

63. What is the typical use for the cummerbund that accompanies your rented tuxedo?
a. wear it around my midriff
b. wear it on my head
c. wear it around my neck
d. wear it diagonally across my chest

64. For which of the following occasions would you typically wear your rented tuxedo?
a. My daughter's wedding
b. I could wear the rented tuxedo to any of these events.
c. My high school prom
d. My retirement banquet

65. True or False: My rented tuxedo's shirt is just like any other business appropriate shirt - button down collar, smooth front, etc.
a. True
b. False

66. How do the trousers of your rented tuxedo differ from those of your regular suit?

a. The tuxedo trousers are decorated on the outer seam.
b. Tuxedo trousers always have a prominent cuff.
c. There is no difference, the two can be interchanged.
d. Tuxedo trousers are always worn with a belt.

67. The tie that accompanies your rented tuxedo this time is named after a town in England known for its famous racetrack. What is the name of this town?
a. Epsom
b. Derby
c. Ascot
d. Cheltenham

68. While you're sporting your rented tuxedo, what attire might your wife typically be wearing?
a. Any of these would be appropriate
b. Tea length dress
c. Dinner length sleeveless gown
d. Cocktail length dress

69. If your rented tuxedo's shirt lacks buttons on its cuff, what alternative method do you use to secure the sleeve closed?
a. safety pins
b. cuff studs
c. cufflinks
d. tuxedo shirt cuffs are sewn closed

70. The famous tune "Tuxedo Junction" was written especially for Glenn Miller.
a. True
b. False

The Bare Necessities Trivia

71. In the Mormon faith, following the endowment ceremony, members are directed to wear a particular type of undergarment. What is the name of this undergarment?
    a. Church garments
    b. Modesty garments
    c. Followers garments
    d. Temple garments

72. In 1995, an undergarment retailer launched a televised fashion show in the United States. The models featured in this show are commonly known as "angels" and are among the highest-paid in the industry. What is the brand name of this underwear retailer?
    a. Tommy Hilfiger
    b. Giorgio Armani
    c. Prada
    d. Victoria's Secret

73. During winter months, and in cold climates, this type of underwear is worn to provide additional warmth. What is this underwear called?
    a. Long johns/handles
    b. Down
    c. Polar fleece
    d. Flannel

74. Some individuals opt not to wear undergarments for reasons such as comfort or to avoid visible panty lines. What is this practice commonly referred to as?
    a. Being free
    b. Skinning it
    c. Going natural
    d. Going commando

75. This underwear company, founded in 1876, derived its name from its three founders. In the early 1930s, it was acquired by

the Atlas Underwear Company. What was the original name of this company?

a. AUC
b. BVD
c. SMC
d. STS

76. **This company, founded by Nicholas Graham, recently acquired the "Peanuts gang." What was the name of this company?**

a. Calvin Cline
b. Joe Boxer
c. Hanes
d. Fruit of the Loom

77. **What garment, primarily worn by men and serving as both underwear and outerwear, is considered the precursor to modern underwear, particularly in warmer climates?**

a. Boxers
b. Y-fronts
c. Briefs
d. Loincloth

78. **What undergarment, intended to create a high, rounded bosom and promote an upright posture, was tightly laced and frequently led to women feeling faint, prompting the need for a designated "fainting room"?**

a. Brassiere
b. Union suit
c. Bustle
d. Corsets

79. **The purpose of the next under garment was to enhance the shape of a woman's buttocks. It was a frame or a pad which was worn over the buttocks. What was this figure enhancer called?**

a. Bustle
b. Jennys
c. Pantalettes

d. Pantaloons

80. **What one-piece undergarment, crafted from knitted material and designed for men, women, and children, featured a front-button closure?**
a. Sullivans
b. Long john
c. Union suit
d. Cobblestone

History Of The Bra

81. **Around 2500 B.C., Minoan women in Crete donned a bra-like garment that served what purpose?**
a. lifted the breasts right out of the woman's clothes
b. drew attention to the nipples by hanging tassles on the front of their shirts
c. smashed the breasts so tightly that almost all women were flat chested
d. made their breasts look like three instead of two

82. **In 1893, Marie Tucek patented a 'breast supporter' that closely resembles today's bras. Rather than cups for the breasts, what feature did it incorporate?**
a. pockets
b. cylinders
c. plates
d. Funnels

83. **For centuries, women endured the discomfort of corsets, which could cinch a normal-sized waist down to 12 inches or smaller. In 1913, Mary Phelps Jacobs, preparing for a formal dinner, faced a wardrobe malfunction with her corset's whalebones and steel rods protruding from her dress. This incident marked the genesis of the modern bra. What material did she fashion her initial 'bra-like' garment from?**
a. rubber bands and cotton balls
b. denim patches and metal chains
c. nylon sheets, rope, and rubber straps

d. 2 handkerchiefs, ribbons and a cord

84. Mary Phelps Jacob crafted these brassieres for friends and family for approximately a year before patenting them under the company name 'Caress Crosby'. In 1914, she sold the rights to the Warner Brothers Corset Company for what sum?

a. $1500
b. $15000
c. $150
d. $15

85. During World War I, the government dealt a significant blow to corset companies by urging women to stop purchasing corsets. What was the reason behind this government directive?

a. women were being sent into the work force and shouldn't be wearing the corsets there
b. corsets were killing women at a young age because of the pain they were causing them
c. the men whom were being drafted wanted their women to be 'bare chested'
d. the government wanted to free up all the metal they could get

86. In 1928, what significant accomplishment did Ida Rosenthal, a Russian immigrant, achieve?

a. created bras for heavy men
b. made cotton the chosen material for bras
c. created strapless bras
d. created cup sizes for bras

87. True or False: Story has it that there has been one fatality due to wearing a bra. True or False?

a. True
b. False

88. The word 'brassiere' is French for what?

a. under arm
b. nursing child

c. big breasts

d. over the shoulder boulder holder

89. In their 1994 book 'Dressed To Kill,' authors Sydney Ross Singer and Soma Grismaijer proposed that wearing a bra may elevate a woman's risk of succumbing to what condition?

a. skin cancer

b. toxemia

c. breast cancer

d. Depression

90. In the 'Dressed To Kill' study, which involved 4730 women, researchers determined the degree by which bra-free women were comparatively less prone to developing breast cancer than those who wore bras daily. What was the ratio they discovered?

a. 95 X

b. 5 X

c. 21 X

d. 17 X

That Suits Me Just Fine

91. Where does the term "tuxedo" originate from?

a. Was first worn at Tuxedo Park, New York

b. After the Aptenodytes Tuxidoa, the tuxedo penguin

c. From the Latin word "tuxadus" meaning to have a tail

d. First worn by Sir James Tuxedor of Blackpool

92. If you were clad in a dry-suit, what activity would you likely be undertaking?

a. Snow skiing

b. Rock climbing

c. Skydiving

d. Underwater diving

93. **Which term designates a series of clashes occurring in 1943 Los Angeles involving white sailors and Latino youths from the local community?**
a. Bahama Suit Brawls
b. Nehru Jacket Wars
c. Zoot Suit Riots
d. Leisure Suit Liaisons

94. **What was the name of the garment donned by women during the Victorian era, specifically tailored for their engagement in equestrian activities?**
a. Clydesdale custom
b. Riding habit
c. Riding routine
d. Pony practice

95. **Which individual was the first to wear the pioneering Skafandr Kosmicheskiy suit?**
a. Yuri Gagarin
b. Jacques Cousteau
c. Richard Petty
d. Lance Armstrong

96. **What type of material was typically employed in crafting a Leisure suit?**
a. Wool
b. Cotton
c. Velvet
d. Polyester

97. **Which of the following items would be most commonly found on a Nudie Suit?**
a. Epaulets
b. Embroidered flowers
c. Hoods
d. Dickeys

98. **What type of suit would you don for engaging in the sport of miniten?**

a. Birthday suit
b. Army suit
c. Tuxedo
d. Diving suit

99. **True or False: Burgonet, vambrace, and greave are all parts of a suit of armour.**
a. True
b. False

100. **True or False: Ascot, cravat, and bolo are all different kinds of vests or waistcoats to be worn under a suit jacket.**
a. True
b. False

A Material World!

101. **What natural material was commonly utilized in crafting the shrouds of Egyptian Pharaohs?**
a. Flax
b. Wool
c. Silk
d. Hemp

102. **Among all cellulose fibers, which one is reputed to possess the highest absorbency?**
a. Acetate
b. Cotton
c. Rayon
d. Linen

103. **What type of fabric, typically crafted from wool or a blend of wool with either cotton or synthetic fibers, provides warmth and coziness to my pajamas and sheets?**

a. Hemp
b. Denim

c. Polyester

d. Flannel

104.   Which American company was the pioneer in producing polyester fiber?

a. Burlington Mills

b. Eastman Chemical Company

c. Dow Chemical Company

d. E. I. duPont de Nemours

105.   About how many distinct breeds of sheep are utilized for wool production?

a. Thirty

b. Twenty

c. Forty

d. Thirty-five

106.   Fabric classification relies on the source of the fibers, which can be natural or synthetic. Among the options listed, which one does not belong to the category of natural fibers?

a. Fibers from cocoons

b. Fibers from animal coats

c. Fibers from plant seeds

d. Fibers from fish scales

107.   Which lightweight fabric is often used in the making of scarves, wedding and evening gowns?

a. Chiffon

b. Cheviot

c. Baft

d. Gabardine

108.   What is the term for the twilled woolen fabric, historically associated with military uniforms and formerly regarded as a textile reserved for the elite?

a. Poplin

b. Serge

c. Velour

d. Jersey

109.   In its unadulterated state, which natural fiber stands as the most costly in the world?
a.   Vicuna
b.   Faille
c.   Crepe de Chine
d.   Taffeta

110.   Which durable fabric exhibits superior water resistance compared to numerous other textile materials?
a.   Gabardine
b.   Hemp
c.   Serge
d.   Poplin

How Do They Wear Them?

111.   BABOUCHES are Turkish or Oriental in origin. How would you wear them?
a.   casually - on the feet
b.   placing them on your head - as protection from the sun
c.   wrapping them around the lower part of the face - to hide the mouth
d.   hanging them from the waist - as a decoration

112.   Male members of a specific profession wear the BIRETTA. How do they typically wear it?
a.   wearing it round the neck, as a stiff collar
b.   placing it squarely on their heads
c.   using a pair of them, stitched to the shoulders of their shirts
d.   pinning it to the lapels of their coats

113.   BOA, traditionally donned by women though it has somewhat declined in popularity. How is this accessory typically utilized?
a.   wound round the head, like a turban
b.   attached to the hem of a skirt, to lengthen the garment
c.   tied round the waist, as a decorative belt

d.   flung casually round the neck and shoulders

114.   During its popularity in the 1920s, how did women typically wear a CLOCHE?

a.   as a padded support to raise the bust-line
b.   pulled down on their heads
c.   stuffing their hands into it, to keep them warm in the winter
d.   fastening it to a belt to hold small, personal valuables

115.   The DHOTI is a well-known garment in India, exclusively worn by men. How is it traditionally worn?

a.   pinned round the shoulders and left to hang as a kind of cloak
b.   tied round the waist with the ends tucked up between the legs
c.   folded into a bag and hung from one shoulder - for carrying tools
d.   as a long skirt, reaching from the waist to ankle level

116.   In antiquity, how did knights incorporate GREAVES into their armor ensemble?

a.   as a substitute for a visor on a helmet
b.   hinged from the back of a helmet, to protect the neck
c.   as long, gauntlet-gloves
d.   as protection for their legs below their knees

117.   How is the KIMONO, a garment originating from Japan, typically worn?

a.   fastening it across the upper part of the body and leaving one shoulder exposed
b.   as an ankle-length robe
c.   folding it and wearing it around the waist as a sash
d.   wrapping a pair of them around the legs to keep them warm in the winter

118.   Where on the body would you typically find a SOU'WESTER being worn?

a.   on the head
b.   across the nose and lower face
c.   around the waist
d.   round the neck, as protection against the wind

119. **How did women during the Middle Ages typically wear a WIMPLE?**

a.   as a veil - hanging and floating from conical or horned head-dresses
b.   tucked into a belt - ready for use as a handkerchief
c.   draped over the head and under the chin - to form a frame for the face
d.   twisted into a coil in their hair

120. **If you have permission to enter a synagogue during prayer, you will likely observe numerous YARMULKAS. How do members of the congregation typically wear them?**

a.   strapped to their upper arms
b.   as long sashes draped round their necks with the ends hanging down in front
c.   on their heads
d.   across their foreheads

Cute as a Butto!

121. **Which French monarch was rumored to have embellished his attire with approximately 13,600 buttons during his encounter with Henry VIII?**

a.   Francis I
b.   Henry II
c.   Louis II
d.   Louis IV

122. **Which faction of English Protestants regarded buttons as frivolous and morally wrong?**

a.   Anglicans
b.   Quakers
c.   Puritans
d.   Lutherans

123. **During the days of the Empire, where did Chinese officials exhibit buttons to denote their rank?**

a.   on their shoes
b.   on the back of their robes

c. on the handle of their swords

d. on their hats

124. True or False: Pearl buttons adorn the costumes of London's Pearly Kings and Queens.

a. True

b. False

125. What is the term for a lengthened button featuring two holes at the center and typically secured through a loop?

a. tube button

b. toggle button

c. horn button

d. log button

126. Which would not be a good choice to use for a Dorset button?

a. thread

b. yarn

c. plastic

d. Fabric

127. What is the name for small knobs created from knotted strings that pass through a loop to secure fastening?

a. hoop

b. loop

c. eyelet

d. Frog

128. In which location is the Keep Homestead Museum situated, known for housing the largest collection of vintage and antique buttons in the Northeast?

a. Monson, MA

b. Trenton NJ

c. New York City

d. Philadelphia, PA

129.   Which is the button that is sewn by running the thread through a small "protrusion" rather than two or four holes on the center?

a.   a buttonhook
b.   a wheel button
c.   a hook and eye
d.   a shank button

130.   Stud buttons, typically crafted from metal and fastened through the fabric using a metal rivet, are commonly found on which type of clothing?

a.   knit sweaters
b.   jeans and denim jackets
c.   suits
d.   evening wear

It's All About Cashmere!

131.   Cashmere is sourced from the Kashmir goat, also known as the down goat. It can be dyed in various colors, but which of these colors is not naturally occurring in cashmere?

a.   White
b.   Grey
c.   Brown
d.   Dark red

132.   During which season does the Kashmir goat typically undergo shedding?

a.   Spring
b.   Winter
c.   Autumn
d.   Summer

133.   What mechanical process is employed to separate the goat's soft undercoat, known as down, from the straight, coarse outer layer called guard hair?

a.   Seperating the fibers

b. Splincing
c. Dehairing
d. Dehairitization

134.   What is a virgin fiber?
a. All of these
b. A fiber that is an unusual colour and does not need to be dyed
c. A fiber that has come from a special goat
d. New fiber that has not been processed

135.   When worn, approximately how much warmer is cashmere compared to sheep's wool?
a. Cashmere is 8 times warmer
b. Wool is actually warmer
c. They provide the same amount or warmth
d. Cashmere is 3 times warmer

136.   Which country produces 60 percent of the world's cashmere?
a. China
b. Mongolia
c. India
d. New Zealand

137.   In the high mountain regions, goats are exposed to harsh cold weather conditions. How does this extreme cold affect the quality of cashmere?
a. It helps the cashmere grow faster
b. It deteriorates the cashmere quality
c. It makes the cashmere better quality
d. It doesn't do anything

138.   What is the typical duration for a Kashmir goat to produce enough fiber to manufacture one sweater?
a. 6 months
b. 4 years
c. 10 years
d. 2 years and 5 months

139.   Where on the goat does the highest quality cashmere typically grow?

a. The belly and throat
b. The throat and the tail
c. The belly and top of the head
d. The tail and the belly

140. **What are the initial and final steps among the five processes involved in producing a cashmere garment?**
a. Spinning and weaving/knitting
b. Collecting and spinning
c. Collecting and weaving/knitting
d. Sorting and spinning

ANSWERS

1. Sewing machine
2. Shoes
3. Gideon Sundback
4. Rubber boots
5. Women's clothing
6. Gaposis
7. Both of these
8. False
9. YKK
10. Velcro
11. Nothing
12. Toga
13. The Puritans
14. Bikini
15. Madonna
16. G-strings
17. It had a deep, plunging neckline
18. Borat
19. Corset
20. Raw flank steak
21. Gabrielle ("Coco") Chanel
22. cashmere
23. Katharine Hepburn
24. Christian Louboutin
25. Burberry
26. Diane von Furstenberg
27. Birkin bag
28. Jacqueline Kennedy and Barbara Bush
29. Jacob Davis and Levi Strauss
30. Queen Victoria of England
31. Tank suit

32. The Vatican
33. Surf Trunks
34. Microkini
35. The top
36. Swim briefs
37. Shoulder straps
38. It features a type of crop top
39. Cycling shorts
40. Burquini
41. Bloomers
42. Corset
43. Petticoat
44. Bodice
45. Waist whittler
46. Stockings
47. Suspender belt
48. Bustenhalter
49. Handmade washable fabric sanitary pads
50. Bustle
51. Waistcoat
52. Singlet
53. Sweater vest
54. Banyan
55. Bullet-proof vest
56. Kutte
57. Jerkin
58. Fishing vest
59. Bouclé
60. Robe
61. It is the name of a town and country club.
62. patent leather
63. wear it around my midriff
64. I could wear the rented tuxedo to any of these events.
65. False
66. The tuxedo trousers are decorated on the outer seam.
67. Ascot
68. Any of these would be appropriate

69. cufflinks

70. False

71. Temple garments

72. Victoria's Secret

73. Long johns/handles

74. Going commando

75. BVD

76. Joe Boxer

77. Loincloth

78. Corsets

79. Bustle

80. Union suit

81. lifted the breasts right out of the woman's clothes

82. pockets

83. 2 handkerchiefs, ribbons and a cord

84. $1500

85. the government wanted to free up all the metal they could get

86. created cup sizes for bras

87. True

88. under arm

89. breast cancer

90. 21 X

91. Was first worn at Tuxedo Park, New York

92. Underwater diving

93. Zoot Suit Riots

94. Riding habit

95. Yuri Gagarin

96. Polyester

97. Embroidered flowers

98. Birthday suit

99. True

100.   False

101.   Flax

102.   Rayon

103.   Flannel

104.   E. I. duPont de Nemours

105.   Forty

106. Fibers from fish scales
107. Chiffon
108. Serge
109. Vicuna
110. Hemp
111. casually - on the feet
112. placing it squarely on their heads
113. flung casually round the neck and shoulders
114. pulled down on their heads
115. tied round the waist with the ends tucked up between the legs
116. as protection for their legs below their knees
117. as an ankle-length robe
118. on the head
119. draped over the head and under the chin - to form a frame for the face
120. on their heads
121. Francis I
122. Puritans
123. on their hats
124. False
125. toggle button
126. plastic
127. frog
128. Monson, MA
129. a shank button
130. jeans and denim jackets
131. Dark red
132. Spring
133. Dehairing
134. has not been processed
135. Cashmere is 8 times warmer
136. China
137. It makes the cashmere better quality
138. 4 years
139. The belly and throat

FOOTWEAR FACTS

A Collection of Shoes!

1. **Originally, these shoes boasted a heel but were subsequently redesigned to be flat. The modern iteration of these shoes is credited to Anna Pavlova. What type of footwear do they represent?**
   a. Espadrilles
   b. Clogs
   c. Ballet shoes
   d. Moccasins

2. **While various civilizations utilized some variation of clogs, they are primarily linked with the Netherlands. What is the Dutch word for 'clog'?**
   a. Smakelijk
   b. Goededag
   c. Gezondheid
   d. Klompen

3. **Many individuals are familiar with brogues, a type of formal footwear. However, what exactly is 'broguing', the distinguishing feature that sets this dress shoe apart from others of similar style?**

a. A term for the way laces are tied
b. A way to tan leather
c. Decorative perforations or holes
d. A method of dyeing

4. **Can you recall "bovver boots," robust lace-up boots frequently donned by hooligans and skinheads? Which footwear brand was strongly linked to this subculture?**
a. Jodhpur Boots
b. Go-Go Boots
c. Doc Martens
d. Sketchers

5. **Espadrilles are footwear frequently encountered in Spain and France, featuring a sole crafted from a rope-like plant material. From which Western Romance language, associated with Spain, does the term 'espadrille' originate?**
a. Romanian
b. Catalan
c. Norse
d. Russian

6. **What is the specific purpose of galoshes?**
a. Protect your shoes
b. Help you climb cliffs
c. Make walking easier
d. Look good at the Oscars

7. **Flip flops, a popular style of lightweight sandals featuring a flat sole and a Y-shaped strap, are widely worn worldwide. However, what is the term used for this footwear in Australia?**
a. Thongs
b. Y-flips
c. Pavement slappers
d. Slap flops

8. **True or False: Up until the mid 19th century, the overwhelming majority of shoes were not made for left and right feet - they were straight, so could be worn on either.**

a. True
b. False

9. Lotus Shoes were specially crafted for individuals of which nationality/gender?
a. Japanese men
b. Chinese women
c. South African men
d. Russian women

10. Since the introduction of the initial pair in 2002, over 300 million pairs of these non-slip, lightweight shoes have been sold. Fashion enthusiasts often jokingly dub them "an effective form of birth control." What is the name of this American footwear brand?
a. Vans
b. Cloud
c. Converse
d. Crocs

Hell on High Heels!

11. Yes or No: Is it true that high heels were initially worn by men rather than women?
a. Yes
b. No

12. The earliest recorded depiction of men wearing high heels dates back to the ninth century. In which country, linked with Cyrus the Great, was this discovery made?
a. Greece
b. Egypt
c. Persia
d. Germany

13. **By the onset of the Middle Ages, both men and women were sporting a form of wooden footwear featuring an elevated heel for outdoor use. Intended to elevate the foot above mud, dirt, and dung, what were these shoes commonly referred to as?**
a. Patters
b. Pattens
c. Pitters
d. Patterns

14. **By the 16th century, high heels had transitioned from being solely utilitarian outdoor wear to becoming elaborate and embellished fashion statements for affluent men and women. This shift gave rise to a phrase we now associate with today's well-to-do. What is this expression?**
a. High heeled
b. Well heeled
c. Round heeled
d. Low at heels

15. **By the late 18th and early 19th centuries, a gradual change was observed in the styles of high heels worn by men and women. Men started sporting significantly lower heels compared to women. This shift has been credited, at least in part, to which renowned French leader?**
a. Joan of Arc
b. Napoleon
c. Charlemagne
d. Louis XIV

16. **However brief the reprieve from torture, by the Victorian era, high heels for women had made a triumphant comeback. What perceived beauty trait in women played a role in this resurgence of footwear?**
a. Bigger bosoms
b. Arched instep
c. Wide hips
d. Dainty kneecaps

17. **For a brief period in the early 20th century, women started advocating for more practical footwear. However, a notable era marked a shift in this trend. Linked with the vibrant lifestyle of "bright young things" and flappers, which era was this?**
a.   Roaring Twenties
b.   Throbbing Thirties
c.   Frantic Forties
d.   Foolish Fifties

18. **Is it true that high heels were once banned from public buildings?**
a.   Yes
b.   No

19. **In the 1960s and early 1970s, which social movement witnessed a resolute campaign not only to burn bras but also to liberate women from the constraints of high heels?**
a.   Racism
b.   Environmentalism
c.   Feminism
d.   The right to vote

20. **Today, the debate regarding the merits and drawbacks of wearing high heels persists. Intriguingly, while fashion designers staunchly defend the footwear, which profession is increasingly vocal in opposing their use?**
a.   Teachers
b.   Lawyers
c.   Rockets scientists
d.   Doctors

Facts about Ho Chi Minh and Other Sandals

21. **Broadly speaking, how does a sandal differ from other types of footwear?**

a. The back is open
b. Most of the foot is left uncovered
c. There is a divider between the first and second toes
d. There are dividers between all toes

22. During which cultural period in human history do archaeologists believe the origin of sandals occurred?
a. Neolithic Age
b. Mesolithic Age
c. Paleolithic Age
d. Iron Age

23. In which U.S. state was Fort Rock Cave, where some of the oldest sandals were discovered?
a. Oregon
b. Missouri
c. Kentucky
d. Hawaii

24. Although earlier findings have since been unearthed, whose discovery marked the first instance of a sandal adorned with leather embellishments?
a. Otzi
b. Cao Cao
c. Ginger
d. Queen Eadgyth

25. While King Tutankhamun was famously interred with sandals crafted from gold, what was the customary material used by ordinary people in ancient Egypt for making sandals?
a. Bronze
b. Leather
c. Papyrus
d. Wood

26. The ancient Greeks sported various types of sandals, with soldiers often donning "cothurnus" sandals. How did these differ from the sandals worn by philosophers?
a. It had high heels
b. It was completely made of leather

c. It laced up a person's calves

d. It was decorated with spikes

27. Which island lent its name to the sandals popularized by Jackie Kennedy?

a. Elba

b. Corsica

c. Capri

d. Sicily

28. For centuries, sandals have been a popular choice of footwear in Japan. What is the primary distinction between geta and zori?

a. The shape of the thong

b. The number of straps

c. One has an elevated base

d. The material used for the bottom

29. Since the 1960s, Havaianas have been a favored brand of flip-flop sandals. Originally, for which demographic were they primarily manufactured?

a. Beachcombers

b. Children

c. Elderly

d. Working class

30. During the Vietnam War, from which item did people fashion Ho Chi Minh sandals?

a. Tree leaves

b. Tires

c. Rice plants

d. Tanks

History of Shoes Facts

31. **Chopines were extremely elevated platform shoes, originally designed to shield elite feet from the filth and grime at street level. They soared to extravagant heights and gained popularity during the 15th and 16th centuries in which city?**
a.   Paris
b.   Beijing
c.   London
d.   Venice

32. **Foot binding was a fashionable practice in the Chinese court, where women wore intricate, embroidered slippers. What were these shoes commonly referred to as?**
a.   golden slippers
b.   peach blossoms
c.   heaven boats
d.   lotus shoes

33. **Who was the shoe designer that crafted his inaugural pair so his sister could have new shoes for her first communion? Renowned for designing footwear for Hollywood stars, he later integrated steel inserts for arch support after studying anatomy. Eventually, he established his workshop in Florence, Italy.**
a.   Bruno Magli
b.   Andre Perugia
c.   Manolo Blahnik
d.   Salvatore Ferragamo

34. **During the OJ Simpson trial, a Federal Bureau of Investigations expert testified that the bloody footprints at the crime scene were left by a pair of size 12 shoes from which designer?**
a.   Cesare Paciotti
b.   Ted Baker
c.   Bruno Magli
d.   Kenneth Cole

35. **Archaeological evidence indicates that shoes have been worn for a considerable length of time. Nonetheless, due to the rapid decomposition of materials used to make shoes, only a few**

ancient specimens have been uncovered. The oldest shoes discovered to date are approximately 10,000 years old. Where were they unearthed?

a. Bolivia
b. Egypt
c. United States
d. China

36. What is the origin of the name "Doc Martens"?
a. Marten, Bulgaria
b. a German physician
c. a skinhead musician
d. a trucker

37. What is the term for the Japanese footwear consisting of thong sandals with a wooden sole elevated on two wooden strips?
a. yukata
b. zori
c. geta
d. Tabi

38. What type of shoe is a plimsoll?
a. hobnail boot
b. rope soled shoe
c. high-laced boot
d. rubber soled shoe

39. Espadrilles, originally crafted by Catalonian farmers and referred to as "alpargatas," have their name "espadrille," originating from France. What does the term "espadrille" specifically refer to?
a. Espana
b. a shoe designer
c. a Riviera resort
d. esparto grass

40. **After coming home from a hunting trip with sopping wet feet, this man was inspired to create the "Maine Hunting Shoe" with a waterproof sole.**
a.   Alvah Curtis Roebuck
b.   Leon Leonwood Bean
c.   John A. Frye
d.   Dick Cabela

Best Foot Forward for this Footwear

41. **What is the original meaning of the word "stiletto"?**
a.   sharp as an icicle
b.   little dagger
c.   the strongest pin
d.   as strong as steel

42. **Which men's shoe style was named after a British city renowned for its prestigious university?**
a.   Cambridge
b.   London
c.   Edinburgh
d.   Oxford

43. **Which style of elastic-sided boots gained popularity during the early 1960s?**
a.   Hackney Boots
b.   Kensington Boots
c.   Chelsea Boots
d.   Westminster Boots

44. **During the 1320s in England, popular footwear styles included "pikes," "crackowes," and "poulaines." What was the most distinctive feature of these styles?**
a.   The toes of the shoes became a sharp point.
b.   The boots extended above the knees.
c.   The heels were built up to over three inches high.

d.   The soles were covered by leather studs.

45. During the reign of Henry VIII, shoes with soles reaching six and a half inches wide were commonplace. What was the term used to describe this type of shoe?
a.   codfish
b.   puddle sacks
c.   flounders
d.   foot bags

46. During which decade of the 20th century were enormous platform shoes dominant?
a.   The 1970s
b.   The 1950s
c.   The 1960s
d.   The 1980s

47. What significant innovation revolutionized the world of shoe fashion in 1660?
a.   The development of multi-coloured laces.
b.   The buckle being used to fasten a shoe.
c.   The use of silver and gold braid on shoes for women.
d.   The development of a ribbon strong enough to tie silk and satin shoes.

48. By the late 1760s, thick heels started to slim down, although they became less robust, with wider tops taking on a more wedge-like appearance. What was the appropriate term for this new style of heel?
a.   The Dutch Heel
b.   The French Heel
c.   The Italian Heel
d.   The Spanish Heel

49. What was the term used to refer to the military sandal utilized by the Romans?
a.   digitus
b.   talens
c.   caliga
d.   Pedetus

50. **What was the term used to describe shoes with an elongated pointed toe, popular among teenagers in the late 1950s and early 1960s?**
a. eyepoppers
b. carpethoppers
c. ratstabbers
d. Winklepickers

Shoe Business - The Sequel

51. **What is an antiquated term used to refer to a shoe repairer?**
a. Cobbler
b. Milliner
c. Tinker
d. Thatcher

52. **The founder of Dr. Martens boots was indeed a real person named Dr. Märtens. What was his given name?**
a. Bernard
b. Otto
c. Klaus
d. Heinrich

53. **What is the name typically associated with a shoe featuring a single strap across the instep, commonly worn by girls?**
a. Mary Jane
b. Mary Sue
c. Mary Jo
d. Mary Lou

54. **Among the following options, which represents the largest size for adult shoes?**
a. US male size 8
b. US female size 8
c. US athletic size 8

d.   UK size 8

55. Which affluent woman, originating from humble beginnings, famously remarked, "I still have my feet on the ground, I just wear better shoes"?
a.   Leona Helmsley
b.   Madonna
c.   Martha Stewart
d.   Oprah Winfrey

56. In 1987, who famously stated, "I did not have three thousand pairs of shoes, I had one thousand and sixty"?
a.   Celine Dion
b.   Imelda Marcos
c.   Diana, Princess of Wales
d.   Zsa Zsa Gabor

57. An aglet serves as the rigid tube at the end of a shoelace, preventing fraying and facilitating threading through an eyelet. According to the Oxford English Dictionary, the term "aglet" originates from the French word "aiguillette," which means what?
a.   Little worm
b.   Small spear
c.   Little needle
d.   Small tube

58. These lyrics are from the song "Lucy's Shoe": "Lucy's lost her shoe and she don't know where she put it, but I hope she'll find it some day." Which artist recorded "Lucy's Shoe" on their album "The Chinese Album"?
a.   Spaceballs
b.   Hogmeat
c.   Meatballs
d.   Spacehog

59. Which type of shoe is named after a tool typically used to extract shellfish from their shells?
a.   Winklepicker

b.   Lobster cracker

c.   Clampicker

d.   Crab cracker

60. **Where was William Mathias Scholl, the founder of Dr. Scholl's footwear company, born?**

a.   The Netherlands

b.   Canada

c.   United States

d.   Sweden

Shoes, Shoes, and Shoes

61. **In which country is it most common to see women wearing "lotus shoes"?**

a.   Tunisia

b.   Mexico

c.   Iceland

d.   China

62. **According to old English folklore, when is it considered good luck to throw a shoe?**

a.   When someone is leaving to go on a journey

b.   At a funeral

c.   On New Years Eve

d.   On your birthday

63. **For which activity are ghillies specialized shoes typically worn?**

a.   Irish dancing

b.   Sponge diving

c.   Rock climbing

d.   High wire walking

64. **Which Canadian city situated on Lake Ontario would you visit to take a leisurely stroll at the Bata Shoe Museum?**

a. Regina, Saskatchewan
b. Edmonton, Alberta
c. Toronto, Ontario
d. Halifax, Nova Scotia

65. Which French brand is renowned for its high-end stiletto heels featuring distinctive red soles, often worn for evening occasions?
a. Lafarge
b. Michelin
c. Christian Louboutin
d. Pernod Ricard

66. One of my beloved songs from the 1960s was centered around footwear. What was the title of this song by Nancy Sinatra that focused on foot apparel?
a. These Boots Are Made For Walking
b. Boot Scootin' Boogie
c. Die With Your Boots On
d. Go-Go Boots

67. In many cultures, doing which of these things with your shoes is considered to be bad luck?
a. Putting them on a table
b. Wearing shoes without socks
c. Putting your right shoe on first
d. Leaving your shoes under the bed

68. The world's oldest leather shoe was found in a cave in the Caucasus Mountains in which of the following countries?
a. Egypt
b. Armenia
c. Wales
d. Belize

69. Derek Fan, also known as "The Slipper Man," holds a Guinness World Record for which remarkable achievement related to footwear?

a.   He has the world's biggest feet
b.   He owns the largest shoe collection in the world
c.   He wore the same pair of dress slippers for twenty-three years straight
d.   He paid $160,000 for a pair of Judy Garland's ruby slippers

70. True or False: Retifism is the proper term for a shoe fetish.
a.   True
b.   False

Shoes, Glorious Shoes Trivia

71. High heels for women adorned with extravagant embellishments and similarly flamboyant shoes for men, albeit with more modest heels, were characteristic of which century?
a.   17th
b.   18th
c.   16th
d.   15th

72. The 1970s were marked by a spirit of "anything goes," yet disco is often remembered as the era when this particular shoe style reached its pinnacle. What shoe style is being referred to?
a.   platform shoes
b.   court shoes
c.   winkle pickers
d.   Mary Jane's

73. During the 1950s, a novel, thick-soled shoe emerged in fashion among rebellious individuals known as "Teddy Boys." What were these shoes commonly referred to as?
a.   Jeepers Creepers
b.   Brothel Creepers
c.   Soft Shoe Shuffles
d.   Dirty Dancers

74. **Another style, which gained popularity in the late 1950s and has endured with slight modifications, remains fashionable to this day. What are these iconic high-heeled shoes commonly referred to as?**

a. ice picks
b. winkle pickers
c. needles
d. Stilettos

75. **What is the term used in New Zealand for the foot fashion created by both the Ancient Romans and Greeks, which is widely favored in warm climates?**

a. Thongs
b. Scandals
c. Sandals
d. Jandals

76. **For nearly one thousand years, the Lotus shoe style was worn in which country?**

a. Japan
b. China
c. Korea
d. Thailand

77. **When did shoe exports to England from the American Colony first appear in recorded history?**

a. 1640
b. 1680
c. 1650
d. 1700

78. **What is the term for the protective footwear worn outdoors during the Middle Ages, considering that most shoes of the era had thin soles unsuitable for outdoor wear?**

a. Plimsoll
b. Patten
c. Batten
d. Platter

79. **In the 15th century, both men and women across Europe wore a style of shoe characterized by extremely long pointed toes, known as Poulaines. Which country is believed to be the origin of this style?**
a. Russia
b. Italy
c. France
d. Poland

80. **Which athletic footwear manufacturer revolutionized marketing and shoe fashion by sponsoring tennis player Ilie Nastase during the 1970s?**
a. Converse
b. Reebok
c. Nike
d. Adidas

Regarding Shoes

81. **While Dr. Martens shoes and boots are well-known, favored by skinheads, and associated with grunge and punk rockers, many wonder: Who exactly was Dr. Marten?**
a. An American skinhead
b. An English podiatrist
c. An English punk rocker
d. A German surgeon in World War II

82. **In contemporary political discussions, individuals frequently label their political adversaries as "a bunch of jackbooted thugs." How did this style of footwear come to be known as "jackboots"?**
a. They were made with jacked leather
b. These boots were very expensive and required a lot of jack (money) to purchase them
c. They were originally designed to be worn when using jacks or dealing with heavy objects

d. "Jacking" referred to the high polish that was usually applied to them

83. **Derived from the medieval Dutch "klompen" and the French "sabot", this durable shoe protects the feet from farm implements and fishing hooks. At one time it was popular in northern Europe but now is normally worn only as part of a traditional dress. It has given its name to a form of dancing that is popular in the South of the U.S.**
a. Espradille
b. Clog
c. Slingback
d. Ugg

84. **This type of footwear has a name that serves as a fine example of onomatopoeia. Referred to as "zoris" in Japan, "jandals" in New Zealand, "thongs" in Australia, and "plakkies" in South Africa, what is the most commonly used term for them?**
a. Mules
b. Moccasins
c. Flip flops
d. Wedges

85. **What is the most distinct characteristic of a pair of winklepickers? If you wish to know the answer, a genie may be able to help. And yes, there really is a shoe called a winklepicker.**
a. Stiletto heels
b. Shiny patent leather
c. Leather strap in back of the heel
d. Sharply pointed toes

86. **The most famous predecessor of this type of shoe was the Zoccoli in the 15th century in Venice where it was useful in keeping the feet dry when the pavements were flooded, although it has been around since the time of the ancient Greeks. If you're the type of person who enjoys looking down on others, this is the style for you.**
a. Pilgrim pump

b. Bogue
c. Platform shoes
d. Kinky boot

87. **Characterized by having no back, in years past this shoe was a symbol of wealth since it had no practical value outside the home and indicated that the wearer owned at least two pairs of shoes back in the time when owning more than one pair of shoes was a luxury.**
a. Tabi
b. Brogues
c. Mules (the shoe, not the animal)
d. Oxford

88. **In the Basque region of Spain, these shoes are known as "espartina," derived from the wiry Mediterranean grass "esparto," while the rest of the world refers to them as espadrilles. What is the defining characteristic of these shoes?**
a. The use of a flat heel
b. No back on the shoe
c. The toe of the shoe is always open
d. The use of a rope sole

89. **These were highly fashionable for distinguished gentlemen in the late 19th and early 20th centuries. Worn over the shoe but under the trouser leg, they were made of stiff white fabric, buttoned up the side, and fastened with an elastic band that went under the shoe. What were these accessories called?**
a. Gaiters
b. Feathers
c. Gators
d. Spats

90. **Until the beginning of the 17th century, the prevailing style of shoe was fastened with a strap or a buckle at the front. However, in 1640, a new style emerged: shoes that laced up at the front. This design was promptly embraced by the students of a renowned English university, and it is now known by that university's name. Which university was it?**

a. Oxford
b. Cambridge
c. Edinburgh
d. Imperial College London

20th Century Soles

91. Which of the following shoe styles was not designed by Coco Chanel?
a. sling-back sandal
b. stiletto
c. two-tone "spectator" pump
d. classic court shoe / pump

92. In which decade did Andre Perugia design the first open-toed shoes for singer Josephine Baker in France?
a. 1990s-1910s
b. 1950s-1960s
c. 1940s-1950s
d. 1920s-1930s

93. In which film did Salvatore Ferragamo hone his expertise in shoe design and manufacturing while crafting costumes for Cecil B. DeMille?
a. Spartacus
b. The Robe
c. Ben-Hur
d. The Ten Commandments

94. Which designer is recognized for pioneering the contemporary platform-soled shoe and stiletto heel?
a. Herbert Levine
b. Salvatore Ferragamo
c. Roger Vivier
d. Elsa Schiaparelli

95. What unique feature does Canadian designer John Fluevog incorporate into every pair of his shoes?

a. long pointed toes
b. low wedge heels
c. flared heels
d. Zippers

96. Which renowned Chicago-based family shoe company, celebrated worldwide for its exceptional men's oxfords, brogues, and loafers, was founded by German brothers Siegfried and Milton, who designed and crafted their shoes?

a. Florsheim
b. Bally
c. Levine
d. Palter

97. Which Italian shoe designer emphasizes the importance of comfort and style in his well-crafted shoes, expressing the sentiment that "If a beautiful woman's feet hurt, she becomes ugly"?

a. Guccio Gucci
b. Jimmy Choo
c. Manolo Blahnik
d. Andrea Pfister

98. Which unconventional British designer crafted the 7-inch (18 cm) platform shoes that caused supermodel Naomi Campbell to stumble on the catwalk during a fashion show?

a. Vivienne Westwood
b. Jan Jansen
c. Jimmy Choo
d. Robert Clergerie

99. Which prestigious London-based family-owned company, founded in the 1850s, has gained global recognition for creating the most luxurious and costly handmade shoes tailored for men?

a. Church's
b. Clark's
c. Doc Marten's

d.   Lobb of St. James

100.   What distinguishing characteristic is Christian Louboutin's most popular shoe line renowned for?
a.   woven uppers
b.   kitten heels
c.   red soles
d.   crystal decoration

Shoe Business: Where Every Step Counts!

101.   During ancient Roman times, which individuals typically wore hipposandals?
a.   Senators
b.   Soldiers
c.   Horses
d.   Women

102.   Which British military figure comes to mind when discussing PVC rubber boots designed for wet weather and muddy terrain?
a.   Lord Kitchener
b.   Vice Admiral Nelson
c.   Duke of Wellington
d.   Field Marshal Montgomery

103.   Carolyn Davidson, a graphic design student, created the iconic Nike "swoosh" trademark. How much compensation did she receive for her renowned design in 1971?
a. $35
b. $350
c. $135
d. $1350

104.   What word completes Christopher Morley's quote: "High heels were invented by a woman who had been kissed on the..."?
a.   Foot

b. Cheek

c. Forehead

d. Head

105. Who declared, "My footwear is designed for discriminating feet"?

a. Salvatore Ferragamo

b. Mario Prada

c. Guccio Gucci

d. Manolo Blahnik

106. What was the title of the single released in 1964 by Patrick MacNee and Honor Blackman, inspired by the footwear featured in "The Avengers," a television series they starred in?

a. "Kinky Boots"

b. "High Heel Boots"

c. "Shiny Boots"

d. "Leather Boots"

107. What type of footwear do women typically wear while performing Irish dancing?

a. Calottes

b. Shillies

c. Gillies

d. Galottes

108. Which French author is associated with the term for shoe fetishism named after him?

a. Voltaire

b. Nicolas-Edme Rétif

c. Molière

d. Victor Hugo

109. What is the name of the device used during a shoe fitting, where your foot is placed on a metal plate and slides are adjusted to determine your accurate shoe size?

a. Julian Device

b. Bradley Device

c. Brannock Device

d. Johnstone Device

110. **What is an antiquated term used to refer to a person who makes shoes?**
a. Cooper
b. Chandler
c. Cordwainer
d. Fletcher

Mad About Shoe

111. **Which option below does not belong to the category of shoes?**
a. Galoshes
b. Clogs
c. Fez
d. Waders

112. **What does the term "bootstrapping" signify, particularly in its evolved metaphorical sense, considering its origin from the popular adage "pull yourself up by your bootstraps"?**
a. figuratively using several people's boot straps to aid in collaboration
b. the making of boot straps
c. carrying out a process or activity without outside help
d. the hanging of boots by their straps

113. **What are the name of the sneakers that were first introduced with rubber soles in 1892 and later became the inaugural mass-produced sneakers in 1917, featuring canvas fabric on top?**
a. Keds
b. Reebok
c. Converse
d. Addidas

114. **Due to the popularity of high heels exceeding five inches in height among European women during the 1600s, what methods did they employ to avoid falling?**

a. Nothing. It was a display of elegance to walk on high heels.
b. A cane
c. A support person
d. A walker

115.   Who was the original singer, and daughter of "Ol' Blue Eyes," who released the song "These Boots are Made for Walkin'" in 1966, a track that has been covered by various artists over the years?
a. Jessica Simpson
b. Nancy Sinatra
c. Dolly Parton
d. Jewel

116.   How did the adoption of lasts, tools used for shaping shoes, in the 1800s revolutionize shoe production, especially in contrast to the previous era when shoes were uniform in shape?
a. The automated lacing of shoes
b. The imprinting of the grips on the bottom of the sole
c. The adhesion of the sole to the top of the shoe
d. The production of right-footed and left-footed shoes

117.   What is the term for an individual who specializes in repairing shoes?
a. designer
b. carpenter
c. cobbler
d. Drafter

118.   What is the significance behind the popular wedding tradition in the United States where shoes are tied to the rear bumper of the car driven by the newlywed couple?
a. A transfer of caretaking from the father to the groom
b. A technique of reducing the odor of old shoes
c. A symbol of getting rid of the old and replacing it with the new
d. A message of future good faith for the newly married

119. **What is the term used to describe the traditional Chinese practice where young girls tightly bind their feet to decrease their size, often leading to lifelong disabilities?**
a. Foot binding
b. Ballerina wrapping
c. Feet diminution
d. Foot confinement

120. **What is a shoe clicker?**
a. An object that helps a person put on a shoe
b. An object that aids in the changing of television channels
c. A person who cuts leather pieces to be sewn to make a shoe
d. A person who cleans and polishes shoes

Rock Around the Croc

121. **What material is utilized to produce Crocs' proprietary foam resin known as "croslite"?**
a. ethylene acrylic acid copolymer
b. ethylene glycol
c. ethylene vinyl acetate
d. ethylene oxide

122. **What was the initial Crocs style introduced in 2002?**
a. Alice
b. Caymen
c. Athens
d. Beach

123. **What is the stock symbol for Crocs on the American stock exchange NASDAQ?**
a. COC
b. CROC
c. CROX
d. CROCS

124. **What are the accessories or decorations that can be inserted into the holes of Crocs shoes?**

a. Jammitz
b. Jibs
c. Jibbitz
d. Jabzies

125. **Which professional tour is sponsored by Crocs?**

a. foosball
b. volleyball
c. frisbee
d. Surfing

126. **What US state holds the Crocs headquarters?**

a. Texas
b. Washington
c. California
d. Colorado

127. **True or False: Crocs are certified by the US Ergonomics Council and the American Podiatric Medical Association.**

a. True
b. False

128. **Which U.S. president was frequently seen wearing Crocs?**

a. Barack Obama
b. George Bush
c. Bill Clinton
d. John Kerry

129. **True or False: Crocs is a maker of golf shoes.**

a. True
b. False

130. **Numerous lawsuits have been filed against Crocs regarding issues related to the interaction between children's Crocs and what other?**

a. elevator

b. escalator
c. treadmill
d. bicycle

ANSWERS

1. **Ballet shoes**
2. **Klompen**
3. **Decorative perforations or holes**
4. **Doc Martens**
5. **Catalan**
6. **Protect your shoes**
7. **Thongs**
8. **True**
9. **Chinese women**
10. **Crocs**
11. **Yes**
12. **Persia**
13. **Pattens**
14. **Well heeled**
15. **Napoleon**
16. **Arched instep**
17. **Roaring Twenties**
18. **Yes**
19. **Feminism**
20. **Doctors**
21. **Most of the foot is left uncovered**
22. **Neolithic Age**
23. **Oregon**
24. **Otzi**
25. **Papyrus**
26. **It laced up a person's calves**
27. **Capri**
28. **One has an elevated base**
29. **Working class**

30. Tires
31. Venice
32. lotus shoes
33. Salvatore Ferragamo
34. Bruno Magli
35. United States
36. a German physician
37. geta
38. rubber soled shoe
39. esparto grass
40. Leon Leonwood Bean
41. little dagger
42. Oxford
43. Chelsea Boots
44. The toes of the shoes became a sharp point.
45. foot bags
46. The 1970s
47. The buckle being used to fasten a shoe.
48. The Italian Heel
49. caliga
50. winklepickers
51. Cobbler
52. Klaus
53. Mary Jane
54. UK size 8
55. Oprah Winfrey
56. Imelda Marcos
57. Little needle
58. Spacehog
59. Winklepicker
60. United States
61. China
62. When someone is leaving to go on a journey
63. Irish dancing
64. Toronto, Ontario
65. Christian Louboutin
66. These Boots Are Made For Walking

67. Putting them on a table
68. Armenia
69. He wore the same pair of dress slippers for twenty-three years straight
70. True
71. 18th
72. platform shoes
73. Brothel Creepers
74. stilettos
75. Jandals
76. China
77. 1650
78. Patten
79. Poland
80. Nike
81. A German surgeon in World War II
82. They were made with jacked leather
83. Clog
84. Flip flops
85. Sharply pointed toes
86. Platform shoes
87. Mules (the shoe, not the animal)
88. The use of a rope sole
89. Spats
90. Oxford
91. stiletto
92. 1920s-1930s
93. The Ten Commandments
94. Roger Vivier
95. flared heels
96. Florsheim
97. Andrea Pfister
98. Vivienne Westwood
99. Lobb of St. James
100. red soles
101. Horses
102. Duke of Wellington

103. $35
104. Forehead
105. Manolo Blahnik
106. "Kinky Boots"
107. Gillies
108. Nicolas-Edme Rétif
109. Brannock Device
110. Cordwainer
111. Fez
112. carrying out a process or activity without outside help
113. Keds
114. A cane
115. Nancy Sinatra
116. The production of right-footed and left-footed shoes
117. cobbler
118. A transfer of caretaking from the father to the groom
119. Foot binding
120. A person who cuts leather pieces to be sewn to make a shoe
121. ethylene vinyl acetate
122. Beach
123. CROX
124. Jibbitz
125. volleyball
126. Colorado
127. True
128. George Bush
129. True
130. escalator

HAIRSTYLES FACTS

Hair Trends and Transformations

1. **What is the term used to refer to a distinctive hairstyle, initially observed by Champlain in North America during the 1600s, which led to a French name being assigned to a tribe due to its similarity to a boar's head or crest, but now commonly denotes a different tribe?**
   a. Mohawk
   b. Cherokee
   c. Apache
   d. Adobe

2. **What is the name of the actress who popularized the feathery layered "wings" hairstyle in the United States during the seventies? She was a prominent figure in an immensely popular television series and was married to the actor who portrayed the "bionic man."**
   a. Lynda Carter
   b. Twiggy
   c. Farrah Fawcett-Majors
   d. Lindsey Wagner

3. **Which cultures are recognized for utilizing urine, whether from animals or humans, to achieve a glossy shine in their hair?**
   a. Some indigenous populations of South America
   b. Gypsies (Tsigane populations)

c. All of these

d. Some Bedouin tribes

4. **Which of the following groups do not have a tradition of men shaving or cropping their hair for religious or cultural purposes?**

a. Buddhist monks

b. Sikhs

c. Catholic monks

d. Hindu (Brahmin)

5. **Which one of the following demanding hairstyles requires "ratting" or "teasing"?**

a. the DA

b. the Beehive

c. the Crew Cut

d. the Prince Valiant

6. **What ancient plant extract, utilized since antiquity and even found in the pyramids, has been employed to dye both hair and skin?**

a. Henna

b. Coconut

c. Aloe Vera

d. Myrtle

7. **True or False: One of the most drastic procedures for hair restoration involves inflating a small balloon beneath the scalp to make it more elastic, then making an incision and revolving the scalp around to put the hair portion on the desired area and attaching it.**

a. True

b. False

8. **What potential advantage do redheads purportedly possess, according to certain scientists?**

a. their legendary bad tempers will help them protect themselves from warring tribes

b. their skin will let in more sunlight and Vitamin D in the short summers of the north
c. they will attract potential mates more readily being easier to spot
d. they are able to learn to play the bagpipe more quickly

9. **During the Flapper era, or the Roaring Twenties, women boldly embraced a new trend by chopping off their long hair, much to the disapproval of their families and husbands. What was the name of this haircut, which complemented the 'cloche' hat?**
a. The Bob
b. The Gibson Girl
c. The Steven
d. The Gamin

10. **Dreadlocks, characterized by matted hair resembling wool, are a fascinating hairstyle embraced by individuals for various reasons, including religious convictions or as a natural outcome of their hair growth. Which religious movement popularized this style and regarded Haile Selassie as their leader?**
a. Sikh
b. Rastafarian
c. Sufism
d. Amish

Hairstyles Through the Ages!

11. **What type of flowers did the Egyptians use to adorn their diverse hairstyles?**
a. Lotus blossoms
b. Hydrangeas
c. Roses
d. Jasmin

12. What product did affluent women in Ancient Greece commonly sprinkle on their hair?

a. Powdered lead
b. Orris dust
c. Gold powder
d. A form of uranium

13. What feature of a woman was often symbolized by the intricate and elaborate hairstyles in Ancient Rome?

a. Virginity
b. Attractiveness
c. Marriage
d. Availability

14. During the period from 1700 to 1100 BC, where were Indian women traditionally expected to wear jeweled adornments on their heads?

a. Sides
b. Back
c. Centre top
d. Forehead

15. What was the reason behind the belief of early Chinese women that cutting their hair was disrespectful?

a. Because it was inherited from their parents
b. Because it meant you thumbed your nose at rules
c. Because it insulted the emperor
d. Because it meant you wanted to be a man

16. Women in Japan have worn a variety of adornments in their hair over time. One unusual one, however, took which precise shape?

a. A triangle
b. A small box
c. A polygon
d. A pyramid

17. What hairstyle, or its absence, was traditionally associated with married Masai women in Africa?

a. It was shaved in stripes
b. It was shaved in circles
c. It was shaved in checks
d. It was shaved off completely

18. What is the name for the large protruding circles worn on both sides of the heads of Hopi maidens from the Americas?

a. Grasshopper legs
b. Butterfly whorls
c. Ladybird feet
d. Mosquito antenna

19. Prior to the 15th century in Europe, what was the common hairstyle among Germanic military leaders?

a. A knot on the top of their heads
b. In a bun
c. Shaved right off
d. In two plaits

20. During the medieval period, what headwear did the Catholic Church require all women to wear?

a. Hats
b. Veils
c. Flowers
d. Miniature statues of Mary

Facts About Beards

21. What is the term for the study or scientific examination of beards?

a. Hirsutology
b. Peculiar
c. Pogonology
d. Unusual

22. The rate of beard growth is primarily determined by genetics, but it is also associated with which other aspect of male human physiology?

a.   The rate of his sexual activity
b.   The size of his wisdom teeth
c.   The rate of his heartbeat
d.   The length of his nose

23. Ancient Egyptians often wore false beards as a sign of leadership. This included designing false beards for men, women - and what other creature?

a.   Cows
b.   Horses
c.   Crocodiles
d.   Cats

24. What additional stylistic element did ancient Persians and Mesopotamians integrate into their highly valued beards, beyond the meticulous care they devoted to oiling, plaiting, or adorning them?

a.   Crew cuts
b.   Ringlets
c.   Afros
d.   Perms

25. What specific transgression led to the severe punishment of having one's beard forcibly removed as a form of retribution, reflecting the profound reverence accorded to facial hair during ancient times?

a.   Theft
b.   Laziness
c.   Sacrilege
d.   Adultery

26. What was the sole socially sanctioned circumstance in ancient Greece that permitted the complete removal of a beard, considering that only segments of beards were typically removed as punitive measures?

a. If one was an Olympic champion
b. As a sign of mourning
c. If one became a eunuch
d. On the first day of marriage

27. What was the rationale behind Alexander the Great's decree for both himself and his soldiers to maintain smooth-shaven faces during his era, deviating from the prevalent practice of beardedness?

a. To prevent enemies grabbing it in battle
b. It was easier to eat a hasty meal without a beard
c. For neatness of appearance
d. So they didn't get caught in their swords

28. During the time of ancient Rome, the prevailing trend was shaving rather than cultivating beards. What symbolic significance did shaving hold within Roman culture?

a. Enlistment into the army
b. To mark a contract of marriage
c. The first time one cast a vote
d. Transition from boyhood to manhood

29. What notable accomplishment did a young man need to achieve before he was permitted to shave among Celtic and Germanic tribes, where the preference leaned towards long mustaches and hair rather than beards, akin to the style of the Beatles at their peak?

a. Kissed his first woman
b. Killed his first enemy
c. Married
d. Eaten the liver of a horse

30. In the 17th century in Russia, Peter the Great disapproved of beards and mandated their removal for all men. What penalty awaited those who defied this decree?

a. Have one's nose removed
b. Pay tax on them
c. Face execution
d. Lose one's estates

A Hair Raising

31. Upon arriving in the United States from their homeland of England in 1964, the Beatles gained immense popularity not only for their music but also for their distinctive hairstyle. What was the name of the haircut characterized by its inverted bowl shape that became synonymous with the band?

a. rag-top
b. mop-top
c. pompadour
d. pouf-top

32. During the early 1960s in the United States, prior to the prevalence of straightened hair among young women, a particular hairstyle gained significant popularity. Women would tease their hair to create a stacked appearance and then apply generous amounts of hairspray to maintain it. What was the name commonly used to refer to this hairstyle?

a. Beehive
b. Groovy
c. Spiky
d. Like Wow!

33. During the 1920s in Paris, France, a hairdresser made waves by dyeing both his own hair and that of his dog a lilac hue. He quickly became a trendsetter, attracting the attention of the fashionable elite and celebrities of the era. What pseudonym did Antoni Cierplikowski adopt and become known by in Paris?

a. Monsieur Pierre
b. Monsieur Phillippe
c. Monsieur Antoine
d. Monsieur Jean-Louis

34. In the early 1900s, an African-American woman took action to address her concerns about thinning hair by developing a shampoo and ointment aimed at nurturing the scalp and promoting hair growth. She established her company under the name Madame C.J. Walker. What was her given name prior to adopting this business persona?

a. Sarah McLachlan
b. Sarah Carter
c. Sarah Breedlove
d. Sarah Hatfield

35. Consider the pungent odor of hair products today, then contemplate the olfactory experience of hair treatments from ancient Greece, some 2,400 years ago! Which prominent Greek philosopher famously applied goat urine to his scalp in an attempt to combat his baldness?

a. Democritus
b. Leucippus
c. Epicurus
d. Aristotle

36. During the Renaissance period, fashionable women employed a rather unconventional method to lighten their hair. To achieve a blonde hue, they would blend a costly spice with lye and then bask under the sun all day wearing a hat that exposed their hair. Which yellow spice was typically utilized for this purpose?

a. parsley
b. saffron
c. sage
d. rosemary

37. In the opulent setting of Versailles, France, circa 1785, the Queen of France and her courtly women dedicated ample time to fashioning elaborate hairstyles. They would secure a "rat" (a wire form) several feet above their heads and embellish it extravagantly. However, this Queen of France met a tragic fate later on, being ultimately beheaded. Who was this historical figure?

a. Marie Anoinette
b. Lady Jane Grey

c. Joan of Arc
d. Anne of Cleves

38. **In ancient times, barbers held esteemed positions within society. During the Middle Ages, their role extended beyond merely cutting hair or shaving facial hair. What additional practices were barbers known to undertake during this period?**
a. surgery
b. singing
c. magic
d. Dancing

39. **In 1974, Olympic figure-skating champion Dorothy Hamill approached her hairdresser with a request for a hairstyle that would keep her hair out of her eyes while she skated. The resulting style became widely popular among women. What was the name of Dorothy's iconic hairstyle?**
a. wave
b. bowl
c. wedge
d. punk rocker

40. **Since antiquity, wigs have been crafted from diverse materials and worn by various civilizations. Which ancient society was known for adopting the practice of wearing wigs?**
a. Romans
b. Egyptians
c. Persians
d. Babylonians

Profilin and Stylin in Europa's Space Salon

41. **What hairstyle, inspired by the mistress of French King Louis XV during the 18th century, features hair swept high off the forehead and intricately rolled at the sides and back?**

a. Pamplemousse
b. Pandemonium
c. Pineapple
d. Pompadour

42. **What is the name of the traditional hairstyle worn by young male servants in a castle, which has persisted through the ages as a symbol of their position and role?**
a. Page Boy
b. Bow Man
c. Stable Boy
d. Goose Herder

43. **The Europa salon offers a range of hairstyles for your upcoming date, but there is one style we do not provide. Which hairstyle is not available at our salon?**
a. French Braid
b. Coronet of Braids
c. Hennin
d. Tonsure

44. **For the "Earth 1960s high school dance" in Europa's party district, I've opted for an authentic hairstyle called the "beehive" from the salon. What exactly does this hairstyle entail?**
a. One that uses many jeweled combs.
b. One that piles long hair up on the head.
c. One in which honey conditioner is used to smooth the hair.
d. One with short hair and cute curls around the face..

45. **During costume night on Europa station, the gentlemen have chosen to dress as a squad from the US Army's 101st Airborne Division during World War II, complete with their distinctive hairstyle: shaved heads except for a small strip of longer hair in the center. Which historical figure or group is credited with originating this particular hairstyle?**
a. Cheyennes
b. Apaches
c. Arapahoes

d. Mohawks

46. **On Ann's first day at school in Europa, our salon styled her hair by parting it from the crown to the neck and then pulling each side into separate bunches, secured with an elegant hair band. Despite not residing in a neighborhood associated with pigs, what hairstyle did Ann adorn on this special day?**
a. Pigcurls
b. Piggydos
c. Pigstyles
d. Pigtails

47. **As an avid rider, I wanted to pay homage to my hobby by requesting the Europa stylist to recreate a vintage hairstyle named after a sturdy, cold-resistant equine breed on Earth. What is the first part of the name of my chosen hairstyle?**
a. Foal
b. Filly
c. Pony
d. Mare

48. **The security officers on Europa's Station adhere to a classic hairstyle commonly associated with armed Earth forces. This style, reminiscent of a Mason jar, is often linked to US Marines and is characterized by its closely cropped appearance. What is the name of this three-word hairstyle? (Think of Jethro Gibbs from the "NCIS" TV show.)**
a. Loose and Easy
b. Tighty and Whitey
c. Bald and Shiny
d. High and Tight

49. **I sought the salon's expertise to replicate the iconic hairstyle of a renowned space heroine for an upcoming party. This hairstyle, which required two hours of daily styling on the Earth movie set, unfortunately gained nicknames such as "cinnamon buns" or "doughnut hairstyle" from Earth's press. Interestingly, it was also likened to the rodetes ("wheels**

on her head") of the Iberian sculpture "the Lady of Elche,"
dating back to circa 400 B.C. What is the name of this beloved
movie character?

a. Leia Organa
b. Shmi Skywalker
c. Padme Armidala
d. Teneliel Djo

50. **Certain hairstyles hold significant historical importance.
According to the Old Testament Book of Judges (16:19),
Samson loses his strength when his seven (what) are cut off?**

a. jaka
b. curls
c. dreadlocks
d. eyebrow hairs

Easy, Breezy and Beautiful Hair

51. **In which ancient culture was it a customary practice for high-
ranking females to shave their heads bald and instead wear
wigs?**

a. Aztec
b. Inuit
c. Egyptian
d. Aborigine

52. **During the Middle Ages, what substance was commonly
sprinkled into the hair of the socially elite to enhance its
sparkle and shine?**

a. jet
b. diamond dust
c. gold dust
d. glitter

53. **For centuries, various cultures have utilized which part of the
henna plant to impart a red color to hair?**

a. bark
b. roots
c. seeds
d. Leaves

54. Around 1715, in America and parts of Europe, what substance became popularly applied to the hair?

a. powder
b. jet
c. perfume
d. Lard

55. As hygiene practices improved around the turn of the 19th century due to emerging scientific understanding of its benefits, which of the following was a commonly concocted shampoo used at home?

a. lemon juice and clay
b. borax and egg yolks
c. milk and chalk
d. lye and sugar

56. What made the hair of the 7 Sutherland Sisters, showcased by P.T. Barnum in the 1880s, so remarkable and noteworthy?

a. It was blue in color.
b. They did not have any hair.
c. They had hair all over their head and face.
d. It grew to the floor.

57. Following the conclusion of World War I, a new trend emerged in women's hairstyles. What significant change characterized these new vogue hairstyles?

a. They were very short.
b. They were very stiff.
c. They were very curly.
d. They were cut in layers.

58. What alternative name was used to refer to the bouffant hairstyle, which gained popularity during the 1960s?

a. the beehive
b. the pageboy

c. the tower

d. the coronet

59. What naturally occurring substance do members of the Dinka tribe in southern Sudan use to give their hair an unusual bronze hue?

a. dried clay

b. feathers from the scarlet ibis

c. hippo dung

d. cow urine

60. True or False: The first hair museum was dedicated in 2003 in French Lick, Indiana.

a. True

b. False

Moustaches, Moustaches and Moustaches!

61. To maintain the desired shape of your moustache during sleep, what can you apply to it to prevent it from becoming disorderly?

a. Snoob

b. Snoot

c. Snood

d. Snoop

62. Charlie Chaplin used this form of moustache to mock Adolf Hitler during his 1940s film, "The Great Dictator". What form of moustache was it?

a. Handlebar

b. Imperial

c. Toothbrush

d. English

63. What was the length, measured in feet, of the longest recorded mustache known in 2008?

a. 10.5 feet
b. 13.5 feet
c. 12.5 feet
d. 11.5 feet

64. Among the Marx Brothers, which one was most renowned for his distinctive mustache?

a. Harpo
b. Zeppo
c. Chico
d. Groucho

65. True or False: The word "mustache" (also spelled "moustache") comes from the Middle Greek term "moustaki".

a. True
b. False

66. What is the slogan of the American Moustache Institute?

a. Serving America by providing accurate moustache information and quelling skewed beliefs.
b. Providing a safe, secure, environment for all men who sport the mustache nationwide.
c. Increasing popularity of the moustache through proper education.
d. Protecting the rights of, and fighting discrimination against, moustached Americans by promoting the growth, care, and culture of the mustache.

67. What event, initiated by a collective of Australian men in 2003, aims to promote awareness about men's health problems by encouraging participants to grow mustaches?

a. Movember
b. Mougust
c. Moctober
d. Moptember

68. Since moustaches have a long history, when was the oldest known artifact depicting a moustache created?

a. 400 BC
b. 300 BC

c. 500 BC
d. 200 BC

69. **Burt Reynolds, often regarded as the epitome of masculinity, famously posed nude on a bearskin rug, prominently featuring his mustache, for which magazine?**
a. "Redbook"
b. "Vogue"
c. "Cosmopolitan"
d. "Vanity Fair"

70. **Which renowned artist proudly embraced her facial hair, incorporating it into her iconic self-portraits?**
a. Frida Kahlo
b. Georgia O'Keeffe
c. Mary Cassatt
d. Louise Bourgeois

Redheads: No, My Head is Not on Fire

71. **What nation boasts the highest number of individuals with red hair?**
a. Argentina
b. Scotland
c. United States of America
d. Germany

72. **To which form of cancer are individuals with red hair most prone?**
a. Breast cancer
b. Skin cancer
c. Lung cancer
d. Stomach cancer

73. **How would you characterize the commonly observed temperament attributed to redheads?**

a. Patient and calm
b. Short tempered and passionate
c. Aloof and cold
d. Laid back and relaxed

74. On average, which hair color typically boasts the highest count of individual strands?
a. Redheads
b. Blondes
c. Brunettes
d. They have the same, on average

75. True or False: Red hair is disappearing and will be gone in a few generations.
a. True
b. False

76. What connection exists between individuals with red hair and their response to anesthesia?
a. They need lesser amounts than other hair colors
b. No studies have been done on this silly subject
c. They need the same amount as other hair colors
d. They need greater amounts than other hair colors

77. Which renowned artist frequently depicted women with red hair and had a shade of red hair named in his honor?
a. Titian
b. Rembrandt
c. Da Vinci
d. Modigliani

78. Which of these options does not commonly serve as a nickname for individuals with red hair?
a. Ginger
b. Turnip
c. Carrot top
d. Rangas

79. **What medieval superstition was associated with individuals having red hair?**
a. They were lucky
b. They were witches, vampires or werewolves
c. They were calm, detached and patient
d. They were potential kings

80. **Which Norse deity, often associated with thunder, is depicted as having red hair?**
a. Odin
b. Thor
c. Loki
d. Aegir

Hair Is My Business!

81. **Is it true that hair is actually dead and the only living part of it is in the roots and hair follicles?**
a. Yes
b. No

82. **Which hair color is the most challenging to maintain if you opt for dyeing?**
a. Brown
b. Blond
c. Red
d. Black

83. **For those with a long face shape, which hairstyle is generally recommended to be avoided?**
a. Curly hair
b. Hair that is cut asymmetrical
c. Fringes
d. Hairdo that is on top of your head

84. Is it true that you should wash your hair every day?
a. Yes
b. No

85. Which actress gained fame for her stylish short hair and appeared in the film "Casino"?
a. Sharon Stone
b. Kate Hudson
c. Nicole Kidman
d. Cameron Diaz

86. What fact accurately describes hair extensions?
a. They will harm your own hair.
b. They can be treated with normal hair products.
c. They can be colored as the normal hair.
d. They stay in good condition for two years.

87. What procedure should you undergo if you desire your hair to appear vibrant and naturally colored?
a. Use only permanent hair colors.
b. Not color your hair at all.
c. Make highlights with different colors.
d. Make it a shiny brunette.

88. Is it true that the darker the hair the bigger the number in color chart?
a. Yes
b. No

89. What is the briefest duration during which conditioner influences your hair?
a. 1 minute
b. 2 minutes
c. none of these
d. 30 seconds

90. What are some methods for maintaining scalp health?
a. By scratching.
b. By blow drying.
c. Best way is leaving it oily.

d. By washing it well and by giving a massage to it.

Some Beards History

91. What was the significance behind Pharaohs wearing false beards in the distinctive uraeus style during ancient Egypt, especially considering the customary clean-shaven appearance of men during that era?

a. The beard symbolized royalty, like a crown does today
b. The beard symbolized a connection to the gods
c. Working people were clean-shaven; a long beard showed that the Pharaoh never did physical labor
d. Foreigners were depicted with beards; wearing one set the Pharaoh apart from the common people of Egypt

92. What cultural significance does the distinct style of full beard without a mustache hold among the Amish community in the United States?

a. Marriage and maturity
b. Loyalty and servitude
c. Strength and authority
d. Tradition and heritage

93. True or False: The "Tirpitz beard" is named for Grand Admiral Alfred von Tirpitz and consists of very long and wavy mutton chops, along with a sharp, pointed moustache and a clean-shaven chin.

a. True
b. False

94. What is often cited as one of the reasons for Emperor Hadrian's decision to maintain a full beard and mustache throughout his adult life, a departure from the clean-shaven tradition of his predecessors in Imperial Rome?

a. He was originally raised in Spain, where full beards were the norm
b. To hide his facial blemishes

c. He wished to set himself apart from previous emperors
d. It signalled that he did not consider himself a soldier

95. In 1699, during the reign of Peter the Great, you find yourself in a snow-covered public square in Moscow, witnessing a disturbing scene where men from various social classes are forcibly restrained by the police and have their beards shaved off. The onlookers are horrified as the men, now bare-faced, endure the freezing cold. Despite their pitiful state, some of the men display defiance in their eyes as they are released and leave the square. What transgression led to these men being punished in such a manner?

a. They had spread anti-Czar sentiments or propaganda
b. They had refused to pay the tax on beards
c. They were foreigners who had not shaved before entering Russia
d. They had tried to escape the mandatory military or civil service

96. Which term describes a beard style that was once popular but is now rarely seen, covering only the neck and/or chin without any facial hair, associated with figures like Nero, Richard Wagner, and Henry David Thoreau, and today used as a nickname for socially inept, loudmouthed, and self-important individuals?

a. Neckbeard
b. Soul patch
c. Mutton chops
d. Goatee

97. Which individual among these figures was not historically associated with sporting a Van Dyke beard, a style named after Flemish portrait painter Anthony van Dyck, characterized by a combination of any type of mustache and goatee beard, with clean-shaven cheeks?

a. Vladimir Lenin
b. Cardinal Richelieu
c. Col. Harlan Sanders
d. Neville Chamberlain

98. **Various terms like mutton chops, lamb chops, balcarrotas, or whiskers affectionately describe the hair grown on the sides of the face, extending from the hairline to at least the ears or further. Which renowned individual became so synonymous with this style of facial hair that it led to the term "sideburns" being coined in his honor?**

a. Gen. Ambrose Burnside
b. Archaeologist Robert Burn
c. Governor Augustus O. Bourn
d. Admiral John H. Sides

99. **Vikings are celebrated for various attributes, including their distinctive beards. Even in contemporary times, the term "Viking beard" signifies a voluminous, flowing style that often demands significant grooming effort. However, did historical Vikings consistently sport long beards?**

a. Yes
b. No

100. **In the 1930s, a distinctive style of mustache gained widespread popularity, closely associated with figures like Adolf Hitler. Understandably, its popularity waned swiftly after World War II and has never experienced a resurgence. What is the nickname for this easily recognizable mustache style?**

a. The painter's brush
b. The pencil
c. The toothbrush
d. The chevron

ANSWERS

1. Mohawk
2. Farrah Fawcett-Majors
3. All of these
4. Sikhs
5. the Beehive
6. Henna
7. True
8. their skin will let in more sunlight and Vitamin D in the short summers of the north
9. The Bob
10. Rastafarian
11. Lotus blossoms
12. Gold powder
13. Attractiveness
14. Forehead
15. Because it was inherited from their parents
16. A small box
17. It was shaved off completely
18. Butterfly whorls
19. A knot on the top of their heads
20. Veils
21. Pogonology
22. The rate of his sexual activity
23. Cows
24. Ringlets
25. Adultery
26. As a sign of mourning
27. To prevent enemies grabbing it in battle

28. Transition from boyhood to manhood
29. Killed his first enemy
30. Pay tax on them
31. mop-top
32. Beehive
33. Monsieur Antoine
34. Sarah Breedlove
35. Aristotle
36. saffron
37. Marie Anoinette
38. surgery
39. wedge
40. Egyptians
41. Pompadour
42. Page Boy
43. Hennin
44. One that piles long hair up on the head.
45. Mohawks
46. Pigtails
47. Pony
48. High and Tight
49. Leia Organa
50. dreadlocks
51. Egyptian
52. gold dust
53. leaves
54. powder
55. borax and egg yolks
56. It grew to the floor.
57. They were very short.
58. the beehive
59. cow urine
60. False
61. Snood
62. Toothbrush
63. 12.5 feet
64. Groucho

65. True
66. Protecting the rights of, and fighting discrimination against, moustached Americans by promoting the growth, care, and culture of the mustache.
67. Movember
68. 300 BC
69. "Cosmopolitan"
70. Frida Kahlo
71. United States of America
72. Skin cancer
73. Short tempered and passionate
74. Blondes
75. False
76. They need greater amounts than other hair colors
77. Titian
78. Turnip
79. They were witches, vampires or werewolves
80. Thor
81. Yes
82. Red
83. Hairdo that is on top of your head
84. No
85. Sharon Stone
86. They can be colored as the normal hair.
87. Make highlights with different colors.
88. No
89. none of these
90. By washing it well and by giving a massage to it.
91. The beard symbolized a connection to the gods
92. Marriage and maturity
93. False
94. To hide his facial blemishes
95. They had refused to pay the tax on beards
96. Neck beard
97. Neville Chamberlain
98. Gen. Ambrose Burnside
99. No

JEWELRY FACTS

It Sparkles, It Glitters, It's a... Fact

1. **What is the apt name for the first piece of jewelry typically worn snugly around the neck, often crafted from leather but adaptable to various materials?**
   a. Choker
   b. Garotte
   c. Necktie
   d. Constrictor

2. **Primarily favored by men, this item is employed to secure the two sides of a cuff on a dress shirt or blouse, serving as an alternative to the typical button. Its name prominently features the word "cuff." What is this accessory called?**
   a. Porte-cuff
   b. Handcuffs
   c. Cufflink
   d. Cufflet

3. **For the next piece, describing its shape and method of wearing it would be all too easy, but you could gain one if you win a major championship or graduate from school. This type of jewelry is also often exchanged shortly preceding a kiss. What is it?**
   a. A ring
   b. A pendant
   c. A bracelet
   d. An amulet

4. **Let's try this the other way round: On which part of your body would you wear a chatelaine?**
   a. The waist

b. The finger
c. The wrist
d. The ear

5. **What characteristic is universally associated with the brooch, one of the oldest and most prevalent types of jewelry?**
a. It is pierced through the skin like an earring.
b. It does not bear any gemstones.
c. It is always roughly circular in shape.
d. It is worn fastened to a piece of clothing.

6. **A Japa mala is a religious piece of jewelry often worn by Hindus and Buddhists. It most closely resembles which Christian item?**
a. A crucifix
b. A bishop's ring
c. A mitre
d. Rosary beads

7. **Jewelry frequently serves both decorative and practical purposes. A particular type favored by European aristocracy, while seldom used today for its original function, was historically employed to validate the authenticity of a lord's commands even when far from the castle. What is this type of jewelry?**
a. A coronet
b. A signet ring
c. A globus cruciger
d. A scepter

8. **Primarily associated with hip-hop culture, this particular piece of jewelry is designed to fit over the wearer's front teeth. What is its name?**
a. Grate
b. Bridge
c. Grill
d. Plating

9. Initially prevalent in earrings within Western culture, body piercing jewelry is now accessible for nearly every body part. Among the options, which material would be the least advisable for the part of the jewelry that penetrates the skin?
a.   Silver
b.   Platinum
c.   Gold
d.   Titanium

10. To cap off this quiz, let's consider the crowning piece for your head. Among the options presented, which style would you not be able to select?
a.   Tiara
b.   Diadem
c.   Circlet
d.   Bangle

Remarkable Adornments

11. The Snettisham Hoard comprised Iron Age treasures, notably featuring several torcs (or torques). Where on the body would one typically wear a torc?
a.   Around the waist
b.   Around the upper arm
c.   Around the neck
d.   Around the wrist

12. Since the 1890s, Spain has been crafting man-made pearls using genuine components. These pearls are named after the island where they are produced. Can you identify this island?
a.   Ibiza
b.   Canarias
c.   Formentera
d.   Majorca

13. **In numerous cultures, jewelry serves not only as adornment but also for body modification. Among the following types of jewelry, which is not typically associated with body modification?**

a. golden rings
b. hairpins
c. lip plates
d. Hooks

14. **Turquoise is a gem that has been mined for thousands of years. Which of these is NOT a place where turquoise can be found naturally?**

a. United States
b. Australia
c. Iran
d. Arctic

15. **From 1923 onwards, brides of the British Royal Family have worn wedding rings crafted from gold sourced from which specific region within the United Kingdom?**

a. England
b. Scotland
c. Wales
d. Northern Ireland

16. **Regarded as the pinnacle of body adornment, burial suits found in China by archaeologists are stitched together using gold, silver, or silk thread. What precious stone was utilized to embellish these suits?**

a. jade
b. quartz
c. coral
d. Diamond

17. **Which of these precious stones, commonly worn as a pendant on a necklace, has its origin in tree resin?**

a. topaz
b. opal
c. amber

d.   Jasper

18. **What are Japanese hair ornaments called?**
a.   obi
b.   kanzashi
c.   chakku
d.   Anison

19. **What semi-precious stone, famously worn by Queen Victoria during periods of mourning, is associated with the town of Whitby in North Yorkshire?**
a.   Haemetite
b.   Onyx
c.   Jet
d.   Obsidian

20. **What striking color is associated with lapis lazuli, one of the oldest stones used for jewelry?**
a.   blue
b.   green
c.   red
d.   Yellow

That's Just Swell!

21. **That sounds wonderful! The piece of jewelry you're describing features a raised relief image carved against a contrasting background color. What type of jewelry is this?**
a.   Taxco
b.   Plique-a-jour
c.   Cameo
d.   Tortoise Shell

22. **That sounds fascinating! You're observing a bangle crafted from a molded material known as catalin. Given its material**

and era, this bracelet likely dates back to the Great Depression. What is it?

a. Intaglio
b. Paste
c. Navette
d. Bakelite

23. **That sounds delightful! You're admiring a short, snug-fitting necklace also referred to as a dog collar. What is the commonly used term for this type of necklace?**

a. Princess Necklace
b. Opera Necklace
c. Matinee Necklace
d. Choker

24. **That sounds wonderful! You're examining a brooch adorned with your initials. What is the process called when a design is cut into metal to decorate jewelry?**

a. Embellishing
b. Engraving
c. Enameling
d. Electroplating

25. **That sounds intriguing! You're observing an amulet shaped like a bear. What is the specific term for this type of protective charm?**

a. Filigree
b. Fetish
c. Finding
d. Foilback

26. **That sounds delightful! You're admiring a coordinated set in your jewelry box. What girl wouldn't love to have three or more matching pieces? What type of jewelry set are you looking at?**

a. Doublet
b. Parure
c. Baroque

d.   Channel Set

27. That sounds lovely! You're examining a piece of jewelry adorned with very small pearls. What type of jewelry is this?
a.   Bead Pearls
b.   Seed Pearls
c.   Faux Pearls
d.   Duette Pearls

28. That sounds fantastic! In your jewelry box, there's a cabochon. What material is it likely made from among the following options?
a.   Diamond
b.   Emerald
c.   Gold
d.   Opal

29. That sounds fantastic! The next item I see in my jewelry box is designed to be worn around the waist. What could it be?
a.   Millefiori
b.   French Jet
c.   Chatelaine
d.   Jump Ring

30. That sounds fantastic! You're observing a short chain with a decorative element and a watch attached to the end. What is this type of accessory called?
a.   Fob
b.   Gilt
c.   Pavé
d.   Eyepin

All I Want For Christmas Is...Trivia.

31. True or False: The oldest evidence of the wearing of bracelets dates back to about 5,000 years ago in ancient Mesopotamia.

a. True
b. False

32. Which design was commonly utilized on bracelets in ancient Egypt as a symbol of renewal or rebirth?
a. Ankh
b. Scarab
c. Cartouche
d. Djed

33. Which individuals within ancient military forces frequently adorned themselves with accessories known as bracers?
a. Cavalry
b. Charioteers
c. Archers
d. Footsoldiers

34. What hues of strings are typically employed to craft the traditional Martenitsa bracelet?
a. Red and White
b. Purple and Yellow
c. Green and Gold
d. Blue and Orange

35. In certain regions of India, what style of bracelet is employed as an indicator of one's marital status?
a. Tennis
b. Beaded
c. Chain Mail
d. Bangle

36. What is the specific term for the iron bracelet worn by individuals of the Sikh faith?
a. Kara
b. Kanga
c. Kesh
d. Kirpan

37. **What function does the Azabache bracelet serve when worn in Latin America?**
a.   Protection from evil eye
b.   Identification
c.   Alternative Health
d.   Social Status

38. **In which conflict was it common for individuals in the United States to wear POW bracelets?**
a.   Vietnam War
b.   Spanish-American War
c.   Korean War
d.   Persian Gulf War

39. **Which material is traditionally utilized in China to craft bracelets, providing protection to the wearer?**
a.   Diamonds
b.   Ivory
c.   Gold
d.   Jade

40. **Who is acknowledged for popularizing the adoption of charm bracelets during the 19th century?**
a.   Maria Antoinette
b.   Marie Curie
c.   Queen Victoria
d.   Anna Pavlova

The Secret Life of Beads

41. **What sets apart a bracelet from an arm ring as their biggest distinction?**
a.   Which kind of metal is used
b.   The location on the arm where it is worn
c.   If it is a sold ring or a type of chain
d.   The use of gemstones

42. **What is the term for the piece of jewelry typically worn at the cuff of a long-sleeved dress shirt?**
a. Sleeve brackets
b. Sleeve links
c. Cuff brackets
d. Cuff links

43. **Where on the body would you typically find a piece of jewelry referred to as a "torc"?**
a. Thumb
b. Ankle
c. Neck
d. Ear

44. **What distinguishing feature do Ghungroos, a type of anklet, possess, often characterized by the attachment of which of the following items?**
a. Bells
b. Feathers
c. Silk worm cocoons
d. Small turtle shells

45. **True or False: When shopping for jewelry you might see the words "karat" and "carat", do not let the different spellings confuse you as they mean the same thing.**
a. True
b. False

46. **For more than 800 years, which nation has been renowned for crafting exquisite glass beads referred to as "Murano Beads"?**
a. China
b. Italy
c. Brazil
d. Tunisia

47. **A chatelaine was decorated belt hook that was generally worn by which of the following people?**
a. A knight

b. A female housekeeper

c. A Catholic priest

d. A baby

48. What is the correct term for the gold tooth coverings frequently worn by numerous young rap and hip-hop artists?

a. Platens

b. Grills

c. Gates

d. Plates

49. What category of jewelry includes designs referred to as hoop, huggie, and threader styles?

a. Tie pins

b. Anklets

c. Necklace

d. Earrings

50. True or False: The earliest known example of jewelry is believed to be a pair of beads made from snail shell.

a. True

b. False

24K Magic Trivia

51. In terms of jewelry, what does the term "torc" refer to?

a. Ankh-shaped pendant

b. A toe ring

c. Semi-permanent necklace

d. Charm bracelet

52. What color of gold can be produced by mixing it with other elements?

a. Many colors

b. Only white gold

c. Only rose gold

d. Gold is yellow and only yellow

53. In which religion is it customary to wear toe rings?

a. So
b. Hindu
c. Amish
d. Buddhism

54. What type of jewelry is a silambu?

a. Anklet
b. Ring
c. Brooch
d. Necklace

55. On which part of the human body is a ferronnière typically worn?

a. On the wrist
b. On the upper arm
c. Around the head
d. Around the waist

56. By what contemporary name is the Tavernier Blue gemstone known?

a. The Yogo Sapphire
b. The Logan Sapphire
c. The Hope Diamond
d. The Cullinan Diamond

57. In which country is it common to observe the wearing of a kilt pin?

a. Scotland
b. Cambodia
c. Iraq
d. Brazil

58. Where would you wear a grill?

a. On your hand
b. Around you head
c. On your teeth
d. On your feet

59. What is a hair brooch?

a. A brooch made with a dead person's hair
b. A French brooch made to look like a young girl
c. A hair brooch has gold wire hanging from it
d. A brooch that comes from Hair, Italy

60. True or False: The Timur Ruby, set in a necklace made for Queen Victoria, is green in color.

a. True
b. False

Jingle Jangle Jewellery Facts

61. What material is believed to have been used for the oldest known jewelry?

a. Mangalsutra
b. Mother of Pearl Shell
c. Parure
d. Nassarius Snail Shells

62. What is recognized as the birthplace of the Cameo?

a. Knossos, Greece
b. Khartoum, Sudan
c. Tirana, Albania
d. Alexandria, Egypt

63. Where did the Claddagh ring originate from?

a. Galway, Ireland
b. Carmarthen, Wales
c. Inverness, Scotland
d. Johannesburg, South Africa

64. What type of jewelry, often bearing marks of "Siam Sterling," is characterized by its charcoal-black, silver, or gold appearance, crafted by carving patterns into silver to create raised figures?

a. Flatware
b. Silverware
c. Nieolloware
d. Filligree

65. Who holds the title of "The Father of Mexican Silver"?
a. John Buchanan
b. Don Jose de la Borda
c. William Spratling
d. Flor Silvestre

66. What is Baltic Amber, a material that has been traded for centuries, with examples of jewelry dating back to around 12,000 B.C.?
a. Fossilized Carbon deposits
b. The fossilized sap from trees
c. The fossilized resin from trees
d. Fossilized bodies of sea creatures

67. Who selected Princess Diana's engagement ring, given by Prince William, as a keepsake when she passed away?
a. It was kept by the palace for the next royal to marry
b. Prince William
c. Prince Harry
d. Prince Charles

68. What does the term "Cloisonné jewelry" refer to?
a. Enamel painted metal
b. Hand painted clay jewellery
c. Filigree metal work
d. There is no such thing

69. True or False: Todays modern practice is lip piercing, but an older practice in Ethiopia was the insertion of a wood or clay disc into the mouth to stretch the lips.
a. True
b. False

70. **Who traditionally wears or wore the ornamental pendant known as the Hei Tiki?**
a. Native North Americans
b. Viking chiefs
c. Maoris
d. Mayans

Circles Unbroken: A Ring and a Promise.

71. **Today, rings that symbolize love, engagement, and marriage are likely worn as much for their symbolic significance as they are for decorative purposes. Which statement is True?**
a. "Gimmal" rings were popular for centuries as lover's tokens.
b. English goldsmiths prior to the 1940s could not sell rings as "wedding rings" if they tested less than 22 karat gold.
c. The diamond was popularized as the preeminent symbol of engagement only in the 20th century.
d. All

72. **How many gold mines were still in operation in Wales at the end of the 20th century, where the wedding rings of the British royal family are traditionally crafted from Welsh gold, renowned for its purity as the purest form of gold found in nature?**
a. one
b. three
c. two
d. None

73. **During the Renaissance, ornate wedding bands were fashionable. However, when Mary Tudor, queen of England, was queried about her preferences regarding style and gemstones for her wedding band, she opted for a simple gold band devoid of any embellishments. What rationale did she provide for her choice?**
a. "Because true love needs no ornament."

b. "Because maidens were so married in the old days."
c. "Because I may be no beauty, but my promise is true as gold."
d. "Because faith, hope, and love speak for themselves."

74. **During medieval times in England, widows occasionally embraced vows of celibacy and donned distinctive widowhood rings. Their children often supported this decision, and husbands frequently designated their estates specifically to their widows under this stipulation. What was the typical justification offered for this arrangement?**
a. They were jealous and resented the idea of their wives starting new lives.
b. They were afraid their wives would be too old and would look ridiculous in wedding finery.
c. Widows who remarried were considered less than respectable, and they didn't want the family name sullied.
d. A second husband might inherit the wife's property, so her children by the first husband could be left penniless.

75. **The location of the wedding ring has fluctuated over time, contingent upon prevailing customs. On which finger or fingers have wedding rings traditionally been positioned?**
a. Right hand, on any finger except the thumb and little finger.
b. Either hand, on any finger except the thumb.
c. Either hand, on any finger including the thumb.
d. Left hand, on any finger except the thumb.

76. **Around what period did platinum emerge as a favored metal for wedding rings?**
a. 1890s-1920s
b. 1940s
c. 1920s-1930s
d. 1960s

77. **True or False: The custom of the double-ring wedding was revived and became popular during the Second World War.**
a. True
b. False

78. **Has the notion of marrying with a second-hand ring always been associated with bad luck?**
a. Yes. Old rings should at least be melted down and remade.
b. No. In fact an heirloom ring can be especially appropriate.
c. Yes. All the sorrow of the previous marriage follows the ring.
d. No. The older ring was probably better value for the money.

79. **True or False: Gold rings of the early 20th century are sometimes found with platinum applied over the traditional gold.**
a. True
b. False

80. **What term is used to describe rings crafted during the 14th to 17th centuries, which are frequently discovered with concealed inscriptions inside, known only to the wearer?**
a. regard rings
b. posey rings
c. pledge rings
d. gemmel rings

ANSWERS

1. **Choker**
2. **Cufflink**
3. **A ring**
4. **The waist**
5. **It is worn fastened to a piece of clothing.**
6. **Rosary beads**
7. **A signet ring**
8. **Grill**
9. **Silver**
10. **Bangle**

11. Around the neck
12. Majorca
13. hairpins
14. Arctic
15. Wales
16. jade
17. amber
18. kanzashi
19. Jet
20. blue
21. Cameo
22. Bakelite
23. Choker
24. Engraving
25. Fetish
26. Parure
27. Seed Pearls
28. Opal
29. Chatelaine
30. Fob
31. False
32. Scarab
33. Archers
34. Red and White
35. Bangle
36. Kara
37. Protection from evil eye
38. Vietnam War
39. Jade
40. Queen Victoria
41. The location on the arm where it is worn
42. Cuff links
43. Neck
44. Bells
45. False
46. Italy
47. A female housekeeper

48. Grills
49. Earrings
50. True
51. Semi-permanent necklace
52. Many colors
53. Hindu
54. Anklet
55. Around the head
56. The Hope Diamond
57. Scotland
58. On your teeth
59. A brooch made with a dead person's hair
60. False
61. Nassarius Snail Shells
62. Alexandria, Egypt
63. Galway, Ireland
64. Nieolloware
65. William Spratling
66. The fossilized resin from trees
67. Prince Harry
68. Enamel painted metal
69. True
70. Maoris
71. all
72. none
73. "Because maidens were so married in the old days."
74. A second husband might inherit the wife's property, so her children by the first husband could be left penniless.
75. Either hand, on any finger including the thumb.
76. 1890s-1920s
77. True
78. No. In fact an heirloom ring can be especially appropriate.
79. True
80. posey rings

FASHION MODELS & DESIGNERS

Fashion Designers In Past And Present

1. Which prominent female designer is celebrated for creating her distinctive wrap dresses?

a. Georgina Chapman

b. Lisa Ho

c.   Diane von Furstenberg
d.   Phoebe Philo

2. **In 2011, John Galliano was dismissed following an anti-Semitic comment. At the time, which fashion house employed him as its head designer?**
a.   Proenza Schouler
b.   Louis Vuitton
c.   Dior
d.   Balenciaga

3. **Which of these fashion designers hails from Australia?**
a.   Akira Isogawa
b.   Henry Holland
c.   Karen Walker
d.   Dries van Noten

4. **Which highly stylish fashion designer is known for the famous quote, "A girl should be two things: classy and fabulous"?**
a.   Jeanne Lanvin
b.   Coco Chanel
c.   Nina Ricci
d.   Emilio Pucci

5. **Which fashion designer, renowned for his edgy and punk-inspired designs, tragically took his own life shortly after the passing of his mother?**
a.   Roland Mouret
b.   Josh Goot
c.   Zac Posen
d.   Alexander McQueen

6. **Paul McCartney's daughter has made a name for herself as a successful fashion designer. While you're familiar with her last name, do you happen to know her first name?**
a.   Stella
b.   Teresa
c.   Christina
d.   Isabella

7. **The iconic black dress famously worn by Elizabeth Hurley, secured with safety pins, was designed by which Italian fashion house?**
a. Versace
b. Prada
c. Gucci
d. Dolce & Gabbana

8. **Who served as the creative director for the Italian label Balenciaga for a span of fifteen years, from 1997 to 2012?**
a. Alexander Wang
b. Cristóbal Balenciaga
c. Nicolas Ghesquière
d. Olivier Theyskens

9. **What are the names behind the Australian design duo Sass & Bide?**
a. Dan Single and Gareth Moody
b. Sarah Jane Clarke and Heidi Middleton
c. Marc Jacobs and Robert Duffy
d. Kate and Laura Mulleavy

10. **Which fashion label is renowned for its distinctive monogram print, particularly featured on its handbags?**
a. Louis Vuitton
b. Roberto Cavalli
c. Chanel
d. Marc Jacobs

Fashion Model Mania

11. **Who replaced Kate Moss as the face of Calvin Klein's 'Obsession' Fragrance in 2005, emerging as a prominent teen model in the realm of high fashion?**
a. Gemma Ward
b. Daria Werbowy

c. Tiiu Kuik

d. Hana Soukupova

12. Before Charlize Theron assumed the role in 2003, which two blonde celebrities served as the faces of Christian Dior's 'J'adore' fragrance?

a. Claudia Schiffer, Erin Wasson

b. Claudia Schiffer, Heather Marks

c. Carmen Kass, Caroline Winberg

d. Carmen Kass, Tiiu Kuik

13. Which stunning lady clinched the title of Model of the Year at the 2002 VH1 Fashion Awards? Hint: Consider her striking "Arian" beauty.

a. Maggie Rizer

b. Karolina Kurkova

c. Tyra Banks

d. Liya Kebede

14. Who were the three women selected as spokesmodels for the cosmetic powerhouse Estee Lauder in 2003?

a. Erin Wasson, Gwyneth Paltrow, Naomi Campbell

b. Liya Kebede, Carolyn Murphy, Elizabeth Hurley

c. Natalia Vodianova, Gwyneth Paltrow, Carolyn Murphy

d. Scarlett Johansson, Karen Elson, Elizabeth Hurley

15. Which of these model ensembles consists entirely of Australian individuals?

a. Elle Macpherson, Alyssa Sutherland, Kate Elson, Heidi Klum

b. Elle Macpherson, Gemma Ward, Nicole Trunfio, Elyse Taylor

c. Elle Macpherson, Gemma Ward, Erin Wasson, Jacquetta Wheeler

d. Elle Macpherson, Nicole Trunfio, Elyse Taylor, Cindy Crawford

16. Which brunette model, noted for her distinctively youthful appearance, was discovered as a teenager due to her unique baby-faced look? She had one of her initial cover shoots for "Interview" magazine, sharing the spotlight with Kate Moss in the mid-1990s. Hint: Karl Lagerfeld once hailed her as "the great beauty of the next century."

a. Trish Goff
b. Christy Turlington
c. Devon Aoki
d. Caroline Ribeiro

17. **Which Brazilian supermodel, famously spotted eating at McDonald's with friends in Brazil before her rise to fame, was once hailed as the sexiest woman in the world? She has been romantically linked to a highly renowned actor and attended the Oscars with him in 2005.**
a. Isabeli Fontana
b. Cintia Dicker
c. Gisele Bundchen
d. Adriana Lima

18. **Which of these women was initially discovered while working at her family's fruit stand in Russia? Her remarkable journey to becoming a supermodel was often described as a Cinderella story. Hint: Consider her association with L'Oréal.**
a. Rie Rasmussen
b. Natalia Vodianova
c. Claudia Schiffer
d. Heather Marks

19. **Who am I? I was born in Springdale, USA, in 1977. I've represented fragrances such as 'Escada Magnetism' and 'L'Instant de Guerlain,' but I'm most recognized for my work in 'Ralph Lauren' campaigns.**
a. Raquel Zimmermann
b. Filippa Hamilton
c. Gail Elliott
d. Bridget Hall

20. **Which of these supermodels did not participate in the 2004 'Prada' campaign featuring doll-like models posed on wicker chairs?**
a. Jessica Stam
b. Jessica Miller
c. Hannelore Knuts

d.   Missy Raider

I Saw Her Standing There!

21. While the term "supermodel" gained widespread popularity
     in the latter half of the 20th century, it was actually coined in
     the 19th century, though not initially associated with any
     particular individual. Many regard which model, whose
     career thrived from 1935 to the early 1950s, as the earliest
     modern supermodel?
a.   Linda Evangelista
b.   Naomi Campbell
c.   Christie Brinkley
d.   Lisa Fonssagrives

22. Who among these models, forever linked to the Swinging
    London lifestyle of the 1960s, caused a significant sensation
    when she wore a miniskirt to a Melbourne racetrack in 1965?
a.   Jean Shrimpton
b.   Peggy Moffitt
c.   Verushka
d.   Marisa Berenson

23. Which model was featured in the article titled '19
     SUPERMODELS' published by 'Glamour' in February 1968,
     focusing on their routines, makeup preferences, personal
     quirks, and the intrinsic qualities contributing to their
     remarkable success?
a.   Janice Dickinson
b.   Cindy Crawford
c.   Claudia Schiffer
d.   Twiggy

24. Which supermodel, known for her extensive collaboration
    with Revlon cosmetics, gracing the cover of 'American Vogue'

over 20 times, had a serious accident at the age of 57 attributed to her passion for motorcycles?

a.   Heather Locklear
b.   Jean Patchett
c.   Gretchen Harris
d.   Lauren Hutton

25. In 1975, Margaux Hemingway experienced a significant year, appearing on the cover of 'Time' in June, being featured on the cover of 'American Vogue' in September which declared her a supermodel, and securing a million-dollar contract with Fabergé to star in their upcoming perfume advertising campaign. What fragrance did Fabergé launch in 1976 as part of this campaign?

a.   Diamonds
b.   Poison
c.   Babe
d.   Eternity

26. Which of these accomplished black supermodels was born outside of the United States?

a.   Beverly Johnson
b.   Donyale Luna
c.   Iman
d.   Naomi Sims

27. While often recognized as one of the supermodels of the 1970s, this model transitioned to acting after a brief modeling career. She is best known for portraying characters like Jacy Farrow in the 1971 film 'The Last Picture Show' and Maddie Hayes in the TV show 'Moonlighting', which aired on ABC from 1985 to 1989. Additionally, which talented woman starred in a self-titled comedy series that aired on CBS between 1995 and 1998?

a.   Grace Jones
b.   Cybill Shepherd
c.   Christy Turlington
d.   Edie Sedgewick

28. **Jerry Hall, a striking Texan beauty, relocated to France after receiving an insurance settlement following a car accident. She was discovered by an agent while sunbathing in Saint Tropez and rose to prominence as one of the leading models of the late 1970s. During this period, she was romantically involved with Brian Ferry and famously appeared on the cover of Roxy Music's album 'Siren' dressed as a mermaid. However, she later ended her relationship with Ferry and embarked on a long-term partnership with another musician. Which of these men is the father of her four children?**

a.   Ringo Starr
b.   Mick Jagger
c.   Elton John
d.   Eric Clapton

29. **Which supermodel made appearances in five episodes of the US television series 'Friends', portraying the character Janine Lacroix, Joey's temporary roommate?**

a.   Heidi Klum
b.   Susan Harnett
c.   Brooke Shields
d.   Elle Macpherson

30. **Which model, linked to the "heroin chic" aesthetic, has also been dubbed an "anti-supermodel"?**

a.   Kate Moss
b.   Tyra Banks
c.   Cheryl Tiegs
d.   Tatjana Patitz

Model Turned Actress

31. **She has a distinctive smile, and was told to get her teeth fixed. She never did and it's never stopped her being a success. Born in 1944, who is she?**

a.   Jerry Hall
b.   Lauren Hutton

c. Candice Bergen

d. Margaux Hemingway

32. Who is the cool, blond-haired woman whose father was a ventriloquist?

a. Cameron Diaz

b. Twiggy

c. Sharon Stone

d. Candice Bergen

33. Which actress transitioned successfully from modeling to acting, achieving a notable milestone in 2002 by clinching a Best Actress Oscar? Later, she further solidified her career by appearing as a Bond Girl, defying any potential career setbacks associated with the role.

a. Angelina Jolie

b. Halle Berry

c. Charlize Theron

d. Nicole Kidman

34. Who is the Southern belle who takes pride in her heritage but wasn't pleased about having her voice dubbed in her debut film?

a. Andie MacDowell

b. Linda Carter

c. Kim Basinger

d. Angelina Jolie

35. Which actress, originally a model, stood at a towering 6 feet tall with striking blond hair? Tragically, she mirrored her famous grandfather's fate by ending her own life in 1996.

a. Marilyn Monroe

b. Veronica Lake

c. Margaux Hemingway

d. Jayne Mansfield

36. Who is the young woman with an unconventional name, born in South Africa to a German mother and a French father, who began her modeling career at the age of fourteen?

a. Cameron Diaz
b. Famke Janssen
c. Charlize Theron
d. Angelina Jolie

37. Which Capricorn actress, standing tall at 5 feet 11 inches, possesses not only beauty but also linguistic prowess? Her diverse roles span from portraying a Russian assassin to a character with psychic powers.

a. Charlize Theron
b. Scarlett Johansson
c. Angelina Jolie
d. Penélope Cruz

38. Who is the British-born actress and model, known for her distinctively waif-like appearance, originating from Neasden, London, and inspiring countless imitators during her time?

a. Jane Birkin
b. Kate Moss
c. Twiggy
d. Jean Shrimpton

39. This model turned actress started off in TV and moved into movies and has been a Bond girl with a very festive name. Who is she?

a. Kate Winslet
b. Charlize Theron
c. Halle Berry
d. Denise Richards

40. This pretty baby started young and is still making films. She has very famous eyebrows. Who is she?

a. Brooke Shields
b. Natalie Portman
c. Emma Watson
d. Keira Knightley

Super Models!

41. Who portrayed the character Zoe in the film 'Coyote Ugly', known not only for her modeling career but also for her performance in the movie?

a. Tyra Banks
b. Claudia Scheiffer
c. Naomi Campbell
d. Gisele Bundchen

42. Which model is the parent of children named Presley and Kaya?

a. Cindy Crawford
b. Kate Moss
c. Elle MacPherson
d. Iman

43. Which model was notably absent from the George Michael music video for 'Too Funky'?

a. Karen Mulder
b. Linda Evanglista
c. Gisele Bundchen
d. Tyra Banks

44. Which model featured in a collection of car commercials in the UK, as well as in the music video for Westlife's rendition of Billy Joel's hit 'Uptown Girl'?

a. Christy Turlington
b. Claudia Scheiffer
c. Sophie Dahl
d. Christie Brinkley

45. True or False: True or False: Sophie Dahl is the grand-daughter of the late Roald Dahl (children's author) ?

a. True
b. False

46. Which model appeared in the movie 'Sirens' alongside Hugh Grant?

a.   Naomi Campbell
b.   Linda Evangelista
c.   Carla Bruni
d.   Elle MacPherson

47. Whose autobiography was titled 'Swan'?

a.   Naomi Campbell
b.   Cindy Crawford
c.   Kate Moss
d.   Caprice

48. Which model garnered attention with her billboard posters featuring the slogan 'Hello Boys', promoting cleavage-enhancing bras?

a.   Yasmine LeBon
b.   Cindy Crawford
c.   Eva Herzigova
d.   Tyra Banks

49. Which supermodel was previously in a romantic relationship with Johnny Depp?

a.   Kate Moss
b.   Karen Mulder
c.   Eva Herzigova
d.   Tyra Banks

50. Which model is the step-sister of British comedian Richard Blackwood?

a.   Kate Moss
b.   Naomi Campbell
c.   Liz Hurley
d.   Niki Taylor

They Helped Design the World Fact

51. Who among these designers is frequently acknowledged as the originator of the concept of the indispensable "little black dress"?

a. Ruth Tarvydas
b. Egon Von Furstenberg
c. Coco Chanel
d. Otto Lucas

52. Which American fashion designer gained fame for his provocative and somewhat lavish television advertisements featuring celebrities like Brooke Shields and Mark Wahlberg?

a. Collette Dinnigan
b. Calvin Klein
c. Christian Dior
d. Charles Worth

53. Which renowned French fashion designer skyrocketed to fame with the introduction of his "New Look" creations in 1947?

a. Christian Dior
b. Oleg Cassini
c. Charles Jourdan
d. Alix Gres

54. Which of the following fashion designers is often associated with the increase in popularity of the polo-style shirt?

a. Ralph Lauren
b. Hedi Slimane
c. Thierry Mugler
d. Emanuel Ungaro

55. Which Italian designer, in 1995, crafted the wardrobes for the movies "Judge Dredd" and "Showgirls" before tragically being murdered on the steps of his Miami Beach residence in 1997?

a. Donatella Versace
b. Gianni Versace
c. Santo Versace
d. Allegra Versace

56. **Which of the following designers has created wedding gowns for celebrities such as Mariah Carey, Jennifer Lopez, and Uma Thurman?**

a.   Vera Wang
b.   Maya Lin
c.   Michelle Kwan
d.   I.M. Pei

57. **Giorgio Armani is primarily renowned for his designs in which category of clothing?**

a.   Swimwear
b.   Childrens clothing
c.   Men's suits
d.   Women's ball gowns

58. **Yves Saint Laurent, the French fashion designer, is frequently attributed to pioneering which of the subsequent fashion trends?**

a.   Bikinis
b.   Tie-Dye
c.   Women's tuxedos
d.   Flapper dresses

59. **True or False: Mark Jacob is the real name of French designer Louis Vuitton.**

a.   True
b.   False

60. **True or False: British designer Mary Quant is often given credit for creating the miniskirt and hot pants.**

a.   True
b.   False

I Whip My Hair Back and Forth

61. After Gianni's passing in 1997, his sister Donatella assumed the role of creative director for his fashion enterprise. What is the family name they both share, which also serves as the business's name?

a. Versace
b. Prada
c. Armani
d. Valentino

62. Victoria Beckham, once a pop star, transitioned into fashion design in the mid-2000s. She gained fame as a member of which all-female group?

a. Spice Girls
b. B*Witched
c. Eternal
d. All Saints

63. Which fashion designer was Queen Elizabeth II's preferred choice and served as her official dressmaker from 1950 to 1990?

a. Charles Worth
b. Jean Muir
c. Vivienne Westwod
d. Hardy Amies

64. In which country was the shoe designer Manolo Blahnik born?

a. Brazil
b. Italy
c. Portugal
d. Spain

65. What was the actual given name of the French fashion designer known as Coco Chanel?

a. Marie
b. Gabrielle
c. Sophie
d. Brigitte

66. David and Elizabeth Emanuel gained widespread attention when they created the wedding gown for which royal bride?

a. Princess Anne
b. Lady Diana Spencer
c. Sarah Ferguson
d. Princess Margaret

67. What fashion accessory is Irish-born designer Philip Treacy primarily recognized for creating?

a. Hats
b. Handbags
c. Gloves
d. Jewellery

68. Which French fashion designer is linked with pioneering the style known as the 'New Look'?

a. Pierre Balmain
b. Jean Paul Gaultier
c. Hubert de Givenchy
d. Christian Dior

69. What is the first name of Paul McCartney's daughter, who assumed the role of Creative Director for the French fashion house Chloé in 1997?

a. Stella
b. Mary
c. Heather
d. Linda

70. Christian Louboutin is famous for designing shoes featuring soles in what distinctive color?

a. Blue
b. Red
c. Green
d. Yellow

Does It Come In Red?

71. **The company named Junior Drake specializes in crafting elegant and reasonably priced handbags. Established in 1994, the brand pays homage to an actress by her son. Who is the actress after whom the company is named?**
a. Patsy Brown
b. Teresa Black
c. Diana Green
d. Evelyn White

72. **This renowned French fashion designer not only holds noble title as a Count but also established the iconic fashion house under his name in 1952. What is the name of this distinguished designer?**
a. Charles of the Ritz
b. Hubert de Givenchy
c. Christian Dior
d. Lucien Piccard

73. **This French fashion designer was the pioneer in popularizing "the little black dress." Equally renowned for the fragrance named after her, who is she?**
a. Coco Chanel
b. Paris Hilton
c. Lizinka-Aimee-Zoe de Mirbel
d. Antonia Belle Jour

74. **Hailing from New York City, which former senior fashion editor at Vogue magazine gained fame for her exquisite wedding gown designs?**
a. Kimora Simmons
b. Vera Wang
c. Kim Lee
d. Kim Wang

75. **She is a prominent American singer who launched her clothing line L.A.M.B. in 2003. The mother of two boys, she is married to a British singer. Who is this renowned "Hollaback Girl"?**
a. Gwen Stefani
b. Sheryl Crow

c. Deborah Harry
d. Tori Amos

76. On February 10, 2010, the fashion industry mourned the loss of one of its own, who tragically took his own life following his mother's passing. Renowned for his unconventional designs and public outbursts, who is this distinctive designer?

a. Alexander McQueen
b. Christopher Kane
c. Tom Ford
d. Bruce Oldfield

77. This young American designer is as famous for the fact that she once dated comedian Jerry Seinfeld as she is for her clothing designs. Do you know her name?

a. Shoshanna Lonstein (Gruss)
b. Stephanie Cohen
c. Elizabeth Kaplan
d. Dinah Bernstein

78. Born in Blackheath, Kent, England in 1934, which British fashion designer propelled the immense popularity of the mini-skirt during the 1960s?

a. Twiggy
b. Diane Von Furstenberg
c. Diana Vreeland
d. Mary Quant

79. Following the tragic murder of her brother Gianni, a renowned fashion designer, in 1997, she gained prominence for her flamboyant and alluring designs. Among her clientele are notable figures such as Elton John and Madonna. Who is she?

a. Kate Spade
b. Donatella Versace
c. Nanette Lepore
d. Norma Kamali

80. **Born in New York City in 1963, this American fashion designer was appointed as Creative Director of Louis Vuitton, the renowned French fashion house, in 1997. Who is this accomplished designer?**
a. Marc Jacobs
b. Bill Blass
c. Calvin Klein
d. Tommy Hilfiger

ANSWERS

1. **Diane von Furstenberg**
2. **Dior**
3. **Akira Isogawa**
4. **Coco Chanel**
5. **Alexander McQueen**
6. **Stella**
7. **Versace**
8. **Nicolas Ghesquière**
9. **Sarah Jane Clarke and Heidi Middleton**
10. **Louis Vuitton**
11. **Gemma Ward**
12. **Carmen Kass, Tiiu Kuik**
13. **Karolina Kurkova**
14. **Liya Kebede, Carolyn Murphy, Elizabeth Hurley**
15. **Elle Macpherson, Gemma Ward, Nicole Trunfio, Elyse Taylor**
16. **Devon Aoki**
17. **Gisele Bundchen**
18. **Natalia Vodianova**

19. Bridget Hall
20. Jessica Miller
21. Lisa Fonssagrives
22. Jean Shrimpton
23. Twiggy
24. Lauren Hutton
25. Babe
26. Iman
27. Cybill Shepherd
28. Mick Jagger
29. Elle Macpherson
30. Kate Moss
31. Lauren Hutton
32. Candice Bergen
33. Halle Berry
34. Andie MacDowell
35. Margaux Hemingway
36. Charlize Theron
37. Famke Janssen
38. Twiggy
39. Denise Richards
40. Brooke Shields
41. Tyra Banks
42. Cindy Crawford
43. Gisele Bundchen
44. Claudia Scheiffer
45. True
46. Elle MacPherson
47. Naomi Campbell
48. Eva Herzigova
49. Kate Moss
50. Naomi Campbell
51. Coco Chanel
52. Calvin Klein
53. Christian Dior
54. Ralph Lauren
55. Gianni Versace

56. Vera Wang

57. Men's suits

58. Women's tuxedos

59. False

60. True

61. Versace

62. Spice Girls

63. Hardy Amies

64. Spain

65. Gabrielle

66. Lady Diana Spencer

67. Hats

68. Christian Dior

69. Stella

70. Red

71. Patsy Brown

72. Hubert de Givenchy

73. Coco Chanel

74. Vera Wang

75. Gwen Stefani

76. Alexander McQueen

77. Shoshanna Lonstein (Gruss)

78. Mary Quant

79. Donatella Versace

80. Marc Jacobs

FASHION & BEAUTY FACTS

Changing Face of Fashion Through Time

1. **In a noteworthy film of the 1960s, Richard Burton portrayed Marcus Antonius, a central character in a cinematic masterpiece that vividly depicted the attire typical of the Roman Empire era. What is the title of this award-winning movie?**

   a.   Ben Hur
   b.   Cleopatra
   c.   The Ten Commandments
   d.   The Last Days of Pompeii

2. **We are privileged to possess a biography of the illustrious ruler Charlemagne (743-814), authored by his steadfast companion. This work, titled "Vita Karoli Magni," meticulously describes the typical attire of the era, including the clothing commonly worn by the populace, as well as the garments consistently adorned by Charlemagne himself,**

which were also prevalent across the Western world during that period. Who was the author of this biography?

a. Einhard
b. Bronte
c. Austen
d. Shakespeare

3. **By the era of King John of England, the portrayal of women's clothing was depicted fairly accurately in which enduring television series centered around the character Robin Hood?**

a. Archery Games
b. Robin Hood: Prince of Thieves
c. The Adventures of Robin Hood
d. The Red, Red Robin

4. **Moving forward to the 1500s, we are fortunate to have an illuminated manuscript ("Tres Riches Heures du Duc de Berry") from this period that offers a clear depiction of the fashions of that time. Is it True to say that it took nearly a century to complete this work?**

a. Yes
b. No

5. **During the 16th century, escalating tensions between England and France brought about distinct differences in fashion between the two countries. Additionally, other nations began to develop their own unique styles of clothing. However, one aspect of women's undergarments transcended borders. Though not depicted in paintings during that era due to societal norms, later mediums such as magazines, paintings, and photographs captured this garment accurately. Known for its discomfort, tightness, and lace fastenings, it is featured prominently in a swashbuckling 2003 film starring Keira Knightley, Johnny Depp, and Geoffrey Rush. What is the title of this movie?**

a. Pirates of the Caribbean: At World's End

b. Pirates of the Caribbean: On Stranger Tides
c. Pirates of the Caribbean: Dead Man's Chest
d. Pirates of the Caribbean: The Curse of the Black Pearl

6. **In the 17th century, clothing became exceedingly elaborate and ornamented, often accompanied by wigs. Women wore huge hooped skirts, while both sexes sported elegantly curled long hair. These fashions are perhaps best exemplified in a 1974 film starring Michael York, depicting a small group of swordsmen fighting for truth, honor, and their king. Based on a novel by Alexandre Dumas, what is the title of this movie?**
a. The Three Blind Mice
b. The Three Musketeers
c. The Three Little Pigs
d. Three Fine Fellows are We

7. **In the eighteenth century, both men and women, especially women, embraced incredibly extravagant fashions. Skirts were so wide that individuals had to enter doorways sideways, while towering wigs posed a fire hazard from overhead candles. Fortunately, as the century drew to a close, everyday attire became more delicate, feminine, and practical for navigating doorways. This transformation is eloquently portrayed in the exquisite television miniseries featuring the beloved heroine Elizabeth Bennet. What is the title of this series?**
a. Jane Eyre
b. Sense and Sensibility
c. Pride and Prejudice
d. Wuthering Heights

8. **During the first half of the 19th century, Queen Victoria ascended to the throne of the British Empire, and fashion evolved accordingly throughout her reign. Skirts became fuller, while daytime dresses generally adopted a more plain and even severe appearance. However, the atmosphere at balls was distinctly different, with women adorning themselves in vibrant and elegant gowns to dance to the music of the**

composer known as the "Waltz King." Who was this renowned composer?

a. Johann Strauss II
b. Wolfgang Mozart
c. Ludwig Beethoven
d. Andrew Lloyd Webber

9. **As the twentieth century commenced, fashion underwent a remarkable transformation, transitioning from the restrained Victorian styles to the charming Edwardian fashions, and eventually to the flamboyant flapper gowns of the roaring twenties. Subsequent decades brought forth the elegance of the thirties, the austerity of the forties, the innocence of the fifties, and the vibrant and unconventional styles of the sixties, seventies, and beyond. On the dance floor at the dawn of this century, one woman sparked a revolution in hairstyles for women when she boldly cut her hair short and introduced numerous new and daring dances into her routines. What was her name?**

a. Elle MacPherson
b. Elizabeth Taylor
c. Margaret Thatcher
d. Irene Castle

10. **Moving into the 21st century, fashion trends encompassed a wide spectrum, ranging from retro styles to futuristic designs, from casual jeans and t-shirts to avant-garde ensembles that push boundaries. The possibilities seemed endless, with some outfits even resembling something the cat dragged in. As science fiction shows attempted to portray various fashion possibilities for the future, they occasionally missed the mark, leading to disastrous outfits. In a notable instance, Marina Sirtis, one of the stars of a renowned space travel series, faced criticism from the press when she appeared in a very short mini-skirt and boots, described as resembling "a galactic cheerleader." What was the name of this series?**

a. My Three Sons
b. Star Trek: The Next Generation

c.   Quantum Leap
d.   Little House on the Prairie

A Century of Fashion

11. In the 1910s, a significant event occurred when an American woman named Mrs. Hart O. Berg became the first female passenger in an aeroplane, accompanying Wilbur Wright on a short flight in 1908. What fashion trend did she inadvertently initiate, which would gain popularity during the 1910s?

a.   Culottes
b.   Hobble skirt
c.   Bandana
d.   Flying Goggles

12. During the 1920s, young stylish women in the Western world earned the moniker "Flappers." They sported short dresses, indulged in heavy makeup, imbibed alcohol (shock!), smoked cigarettes (gasp!), danced with abandon (horror!), and even dared to drive cars (Arrest that woman!). But why were they dubbed "Flappers"?

a.   It was a style of hat
b.   They talked very rapidly
c.   Their skirts flapped up when they danced or ran
d.   They carried handbags with open flaps

13. In the 1930s, Coco Chanel is widely regarded as the fashion icon of the era. However, she faced formidable competition from a prominent Italian counterpart who was equally skilled in the realm of fashion during this period. What was her name?

a.   Elsa Schiaparelli
b.   Carla Carbonara
c.   Bettina Bolognese
d.   Anna Risotti

14. During the 1940s, what specific body part was accentuated by additional padding in clothing for both men and women?

a. Breasts
b. Shoulders
c. Hips
d. Wrists

15. Which among the following styles, above all others, epitomized female fashion during the 1950s?

a. Poodle skirts
b. Pomeranian pleats
c. Labrador levis
d. Samoyed shoes

16. Transitioning to the sixties, an era characterized by rebellion, freedom of expression, and a countercultural ethos, epitomized by spaced-out individuals mesmerized by candles. Which band, symbolizing this entire epoch, popularized a new hairstyle for men and boys during this time?

a. Frank Sinatra and the Singalongs
b. The Beatles
c. Slim Dusty and the Cow Pats
d. Pavarotti and the Pizzas

17. As the 1970s progressed, fashion trends became increasingly extravagant and eccentric, albeit more influenced by fashion authorities. Consequently, the diverse array of outfits became more refined, with a deliberate rebellious flair. Among the following options, which form of footwear garnered significant attention in the 1970s?

a. Ballet slippers
b. Platform shoes
c. Wellington boots
d. Booties

18. Thanks to the dance frenzy sparked by the 1983 film "Flashdance," which of the following options emerged as a

prominent fashion item, donned by individuals of all body types during the 1980s?

a. Bustles
b. Hooped skirts
c. Bonnets
d. Leg warmers

19. **The 1990s introduced a stark departure in fashion from the eccentric and audacious styles of the 1980s. The prevailing aesthetic during this period was characterized by which singular word?**

a. Dunge
b. Lunge
c. Grunge
d. Sponge

20. **The initial decade of fashion in the 21st century has been coined as "the mash-up decade," characterized by the amalgamation of styles from previous eras. During this time, a specific facial trend gained popularity among men, prompting many individuals to reach for a shaver. What was this fashion trend?**

a. Oiled moustaches
b. The unshaven look
c. Goatees
d. Plaited beards

Fashion Impossible!

21. **Richard Blackwell, an American fashion critic, infamously likened this Hollywood star's figure and attire to the "rebirth of the zeppelin," a less than flattering comparison. In 1965, she famously adorned a 'lovely' blue sparkly dress with an impossibly impractical matching headdress, resembling a fusion of flowers and sticks (or, from afar, hypodermic needles). Who is this actress, known for her numerous marriages?**

a. Katharine Hepburn

b. Zsa Zsa Gabor

c. Elizabeth Taylor

d. Pamela Anderson

22. Who caused a scene on her Blond Ambition tour (in the 1990s) with a Jean Paul Gaultier impossibly impractical pointy bra?

a. Deborah Harry

b. Lady Gaga

c. Britney Spears

d. Madonna

23. Which supermodel, notorious for her difficult demeanor, experienced a tumble on the catwalk during a Vivienne Westwood runway show in 1993 due to the near-impossibility of walking in her ten-inch platform shoes?

a. Agyness Deyn

b. Kate Moss

c. Naomi Campbell

d. Emma Bunton

24. Since the late twentieth century, wearing animal-derived materials like leathers and furs has been widely criticized in the fashion world. However, one Icelandic singer caused quite a stir by donning an animal replica at the Academy Awards (Oscars) in 2001. Who was this controversial figure?

a. Emiliana Torrini

b. Megas

c. Bjork

d. Bubbi Morthens

25. At the London premiere of the movie 'Four Weddings and a Funeral' in 1994, a now-iconic 'safety pin' dress made its debut. Who was the relatively unknown actress who daringly wore this dress (barely!)?

a. Pamela Anderson

b. Elizabeth Hurley

c. Andie MacDowell

d. Julia Roberts

26. While wearing a facemask in public during a bird or swine flu outbreak might seem commonplace, it has not typically been regarded as a fashion statement. However, which celebrity ensured that his three children wore facemasks or veils in public to avoid recognition and maintain a sense of normalcy in their lives? This entertainer also sported facemasks in public himself before his death in 2009, although the exact reasons remain unclear.

a. Patrick Swayze
b. John Travolta
c. David Carradine
d. Michael Jackson

27. Once again, she made a bold fashion statement. Following her daring choice of a Dolce & Gabbana see-through lace dress (with very little underneath) at the 2001 MTV Video Music Awards (VMA), which celebrity starlet opted for a similar ensemble at the same awards ceremony in 2010?

a. Britney Spears
b. Christina Aguilera
c. Jessica Simpson
d. Lady Gaga

28. Could a 43-year-old woman pull off a fishnet body stocking and look good? That's up for debate. Just ask this celebrity who, in hindsight, might have wished she could turn back time and rethink her outfit choice before filming the music video for her 1989 chart-topping hit.

a. Bette Midler
b. Madonna
c. Cher
d. Aretha Franklin

29. Which celebrity, gaining widespread attention in the mid-2000s, became renowned for her outrageously wild hair and eccentric outfits? She further solidified her fashion-forward image by releasing a song titled 'Fashion' in 2009, which was

featured on the soundtrack of the film 'Confessions of a Shopaholic.'

a. Bjork
b. Lady Gaga
c. Cher
d. Amy Winehouse

30. It's hard to stifle a laugh at the sight of the mankini, a male counterpart to the bikini swimsuit. Which celebrity infamously brought attention to this fashion faux pas by donning a neon green mankini at the 2006 Cannes Film Festival to promote his new film 'Borat: Cultural Learnings of America for Make Benefit Glorious Nation of Kazakhstan'?

a. Ken Davitian
b. Sacha Baron Cohen
c. Nursultan Tuyakbay
d. Ilham Aliyev

Consumers of a Certain Age

31. After the austerity of the First World War, the 1920s witnessed a shift in women's fashion and behavior. What term was used to describe the youthful consumers who sported bobbed hair, shift-like dresses, and cloche hats?

a. Bubble Girls
b. Flapper Girls
c. Popsicle Girls
d. It Girls

32. A timeless staple in the fashion industry, recognized by consumers of various ages, is the classic "Little Black Dress." Which designer is credited with popularizing this iconic and versatile garment?

a. Coco Chanel
b. Yves Saint Laurent
c. Christian Dior
d. Elsa Schiaparelli

33. **Individuals of a certain age, particularly those around the 1970s, may recall a peculiar fad that captivated the fashion scene. What was the term used to describe the jewelry piece intended to reflect the wearer's emotional state by changing color?**
a.   Temper Bracelets
b.   Mood Rings
c.   Passion Straps
d.   Blues Bands

34. **Individuals who reached a certain age in the 1960s likely have vivid memories of the iconic miniskirt, frequently paired with a particular type of footwear known as what?**
a.   Stay-Stay Boots
b.   Go-Go Boots
c.   Dancing Boots
d.   Wellington Boots

35. **A timeless fashion trend of the 1960s, this hairstyle was famously worn by icons like Audrey Hepburn and Dusty Springfield, and later revived by Amy Winehouse. What is this enduring hairstyle?**
a.   Snake Swirl
b.   Waspnest
c.   Beehive
d.   Poodle Perm

36. **If you were a male consumer of a certain age in the 1980s, your leisure look was probably dominated by the fashion worn by Don Johnson and Philip Michael Thomas in which popular TV show?**
a.   Starsky and Hutch
b.   Hill Street Blues
c.   Miami Vice
d.   Dallas

37. **What term was coined to describe the descendant of the tracksuit, which became prevalent in the 1980s and was**

characterized by shiny fabrics and vibrant, eye-catching colors?

a. Shell Suit
b. Quick Fit Suit
c. Winkle Suit
d. Cuddly Suit

38. The 1980s were all about consumerism and the fashion of the day reflected this trend. What was the name given to this style of dressing?

a. Power Dressing
b. Capable Clothing
c. Authoritative Attire
d. Competent Costume

39. In the 1300s, individuals of a certain age often relied on "kabkabs" to protect their feet from moisture and prevent their hems from getting soiled. What is the contemporary fashion equivalent of a "kabkab"?

a. Ballet Slippers
b. Thongs
c. Mocassins
d. Platforms

40. Since its inception in 1871, what fashion item has evolved into a timeless staple in the wardrobes of millions of individuals of a certain age worldwide?

a. Nehru Jacket
b. Bathing Suit
c. Overcoat
d. Jeans

Flashes of Fashion from the Roaring 20s

41. **Fashion and cosmetics revolutionized the world following the austerity of the war years. What close-fitting, bell-shaped hat became all the rage in the roaring twenties, symbolizing the spirit of the decade?**
a. Cartwheel
b. Toque
c. Suiter
d. Cloche

42. **The exuberant Jazz Age of the Roaring Twenties inspired young people to embrace dancing, necessitating changes in clothing to accommodate this new lifestyle. Which one of the following fashion changes did *NOT* take place during the '20s?**
a. Dress and skirt hems were shorter
b. Glossy fabrics mirrored light
c. Embellishments on dresses such as fringe threads
d. Stiff petticoats to 'puff out' the skirt

43. **In 1926, Vogue magazine famously compared the latest creation of which French fashion designer, a black dress, to the Model T Ford?**
a. Elsa Schiaparelli
b. Gabrielle (Coco) Chanel
c. Jean Patou
d. Florrie Westwood

44. **Where was the "finger wave," a popular hairstyle in the 1920s, commonly seen?**
a. On the gloves
b. Around the neckline
c. Around the waist
d. On the head

45. **Fashion in underwear underwent significant changes in the 1920s. Which one of the following was *NOT* a characteristic of underwear during this era?**
a. Cami knickers
b. Ribbed corset

c. Four sectioned lace bandeau bra

d. Lastex girdles

46. In the Far East, the Roaring Twenties left its imprint as well. A traditional dress received a modern makeover, adopting a more form-fitting style, which became the trend among women in 1920s Shanghai. What was the name of this dress, which is the only Chinese garment listed?

a. Hanbok

b. Qipao

c. Kimono

d. Kebaya

47. After World War I, cosmetics played a role in helping women recover from the horrors of war, allowing them to assert their newfound sense of feminine power. Which of the following options was *NOT* a characteristic of a cosmetics look from the '20s?

a. Very pale pinks lipsticks outlined with a pencil

b. Ivory pale skin

c. Bow-shaped lips

d. Mascara on eyelashes

48. During the 1920s, rhinestones, named for their purported origin on the Rhine River, gained popularity as "bling" thanks to Coco Chanel. Who was the inventor of rhinestones?

a. Coco Chanel

b. Daniel Swarovski

c. Fred Harvey

d. Lorenzo Hubbell

49. Which iconic hat of the 1920s, later associated with the era's gangsters, originally began its life as a symbol of feminism, worn by the actress Sarah Bernhardt in the 1880s?

a. Bowler

b. Fedora

c. Beret

d. Top

50. **During the 1920s, spectator shoes were popular among men. What was the primary characteristic of spectator shoes?**
a. Non-slip and waterproof
b. No laces
c. Had decorated heels
d. Had two colours

1980s Fashion & Beauty

51. **In the late 1980s, denim was predominantly worn in a particular color. If you couldn't afford to buy new jeans, what color could you dye last year's blue jeans to give them a fresh look?**
a. tye dye
b. black
c. white
d. acid-washed

52. **Regarding jeans, what was considered a fashionable accessory to adorn the front of your jean jacket, hats, backpacks, or purse straps during this time? The more you had of these, the cooler you were perceived to be.**
a. stickers
b. flowers
c. patches
d. Buttons

53. **This hair clip was an essential accessory, regardless of the length of your hair. In fact, if your hair wasn't long enough, you might even let it grow just to achieve this cool look! What hair accessory transformed your hair into a vertical mane?**
a. side combs
b. banana clip
c. big barettes
d. head bands

54. Which unisex footwear, symbolizing aggression, power, and strength, was particularly favored by punk rockers?
a. Doc Martins
b. Work boots
c. Combat boots
d. Rebok sneakers

55. Oh, the experimentation we did with our hair! We twisted, dyed, streaked, and shaved it in all sorts of ways. What was the edgy hairstyle we achieved by burning zig-zag patterns into our hair, giving it a "foxy" look?
a. crimping
b. ironing
c. curling
d. Braiding

56. These very popular shoes were orthopedically poor but financially easy. What was the name of these flat black shoes?
a. Penny Loafers
b. China Flats
c. Capezios
d. Candies

57. These pants were favored by muscular individuals, typically with bulging biceps. You couldn't help but notice them striding down the street in vibrant zebra or Picasso-style patterns. What type of pants, featuring an elastic waist and ankles, were designed to "Pump you up"?
a. Happy Pants
b. Clown Pants
c. Bozo Pants
d. Muscle Pants

58. You felt like you belonged on Miami Vice when you sported these ultra-sleek, collapsible sunglasses. The name of the sunglasses was stamped in the upper corner of the oversized, mirrored lenses. What sports car were they named after?
a. Ferrari
b. Mercedes

c. BMW

d. Porsche

59. **Remember the excitement of getting your driver's permit? The first thing you had to do was get a fancy license plate to display in the back window. These plates typically featured artwork such as a palm tree, flamingo, unicorn, or heart with your boyfriend's name. What type of art adorned these flashy plates?**

a. Air brushed

b. Finger brushed

c. Water brushed

d. Wind brushed

60. **If you were seen strolling on the boardwalk with one of these charms dangling from a leather rope around your neck, you were considered "too cool." What charm did the hot rocker Jon Bon Jovi sport around his neck in the early '80s?**

a. Superman

b. Shark's Tooth

c. Seashell

d. Rock On

Fashion Through Time

61. **When did the concept of individuality in fashion design start to emerge?**

a. 1800

b. 1700

c. 2000

d. 1980

62. **Who invented the 'Spinning Jenny' in 1764?**

a. Edmund Cartwright - a person who worked with looms

b. Johan Sebastian Bach - a famous musician

c. James Hargreaves - A British spinner

d. John Kay - an English spinner

63. Which singer gained popularity in the 1950s through their music and also influenced fashion trends?
a. Marilyn Monroe
b. Elvis Presley
c. James Dean
d. Joan Baez

64. In the 1940's which designer had the biggest impact on fashion?
a. Charles James
b. Christian Dior
c. Yves Saint Laurent
d. Mary Quant

65. What is considered the Fashion Capital of the world?
a. Paris
b. Milan
c. New York City
d. London

66. What is the term for the plastic or wooden structures used to display clothing?
a. Nothing
b. Squares
c. Forms
d. Shapes

67. Who is a renowned fashion designer hailing from South Africa?
a. James Dean
b. Christian Barnard
c. Gianni Versace
d. Mark Eisen

68. During the Victorian Era, which spanned from the 19th to the early 20th century, what was the customary attire for women?
a. Gazar feather skirts in silk and linen
b. Khakis and t-shirts

c. Corsets with hoop skirts
d. Balloon skirts and Embroidered blouses

69. Where was Gianni Versace born?
a. Paris, France
b. Bonn, Germany
c. Lyons, France
d. Calabria, Italy

70. What is the term for the objects and materials utilized to construct a window display?
a. Tools
b. Mannequins
c. Props
d. Merchandise

71. How do fashion designers typically showcase their latest clothing collections?
a. By shouting out from their warehouse
b. Through magazine commercials
c. By advertising through billboards
d. By doing fashion shows

72. Whose 'Flapper Dress' created a sensation in 1925?
a. Coco Chanel
b. Jean Patou
c. Edward Molyneux
d. Scott Fitzgerald

73. In which year did the era of 'flappers' emerge?
a. 1920
b. 1910
c. 1945
d. 1930

74. What is the term in French for 'Ready-To-Wear' clothing?
a. Silhouette
b. Haute Couture
c. Pret-a-porter
d. Bouffant Pret-Couture

75. Where was the location of the world's inaugural glass runway construction?

a.   New York - USA
b.   Paris - France
c.   Johannesburg - South Africa
d.   Rome – Italy

70s Fashion & Beauty

76. You washed your hair with this shampoo because using beer was the cool thing to do. Which shampoo gave your hair body & bounce, but didn't get you drunk?

a.   "Breck"
b.   "Prell"
c.   "Body On Tap"
d.   "Herbal Essence"

77. Speaking of shampoo, this one had a catchy name; "Gee, Your Hair Smells _____". How would your hair smell if you used this shampoo?

a.   Great
b.   Terrific
c.   Wonderful
d.   Outrageous

78. This footwear became a must-have item, originating as a jazz dance slipper before gaining popularity on the streets. Collecting them in every available color became a fashion trend. What were these shoes called?

a.   "Candies"
b.   "Capezio"
c.   "Danskin"
d.   "Hush Puppies"

79. These popular short shorts were adored by girls for their ability to elongate their legs, featuring side slits and rounded corners. What type of shorts would captivate the attention of guys?

a. "Daisy Dukes"
b. "Dolphins"
c. "Hip Huggers"
d. "Whales"

80. **Every teenage girl felt compelled to own this lip-plumping gloss. Among the options listed, which one wasn't a flavor offered by Bonnie Bell's Lip Smacker?**
a. Dr. Pepper
b. Orange Crush
c. 7-Up
d. Mt. Dew

81. **Which of the following products transformed kids into their favorite superhero or cartoon character?**
a. PowerPants
b. HeroBriefs
c. Underoos
d. SuperSlips

82. **Which perfume, still in production, was known for transforming girls into sophisticated women with its alluring scent? Often applied liberally before heading off to school, this fragrance, introduced in 1993, even offered variations in Blue and Red.**
a. "Love's Baby Soft"
b. "Charlie"
c. "Emerude"
d. "Jean Nate"

83. **What Maybelline product was a must-have for every girl, constantly reapplied every 5 minutes for maximum shine? Whether preparing for a chance encounter with a crush or simply aiming for that perfect glossy look, this lip gloss was an essential part of many routines.**
a. "Lip Smackers"
b. "Kissing Potion"
c. "Pocket Goo"
d. "Smudge Pots"

84. **Which vibrant pants were the ultimate choice for standing out and looking absolutely dynamite under the dazzling lights of the disco or roller rink? These pants were guaranteed to steal the show and shine brilliantly beneath the glowing disco ball.**
a. "Satin Pants"
b. "Toughskins"
c. "Leggins"
d. "Levis"

85. **Which "Fabergé" aftershave introduced young boys to the world of shaving, offering a glimpse into their future routines? Known for its raw and rugged scent, this aftershave, also favored by the iconic Joe Namath, embodied masculinity and sophistication.**
a. "Aqua Velva"
b. "Old Spice"
c. "Brut for Men"
d. "Stetson"

History of Fashion - Did We Really Wear That?

86. **What garment from the 17th century is known as a farthingale?**
a. A cape worn around the shoulders of both sexes for warmth
b. A large wired lace collar
c. A wide hoop worn under ladies' gowns
d. A type of bag used for travelling

87. **In the context of the 17th century, what distinctive characteristics would help you identify a Roundhead?**
a. Dress was sombre, modest and dark
b. Ribbons, bows and bright colours were absent
c. Hair was cut close fairly to the head
d. All of these

88. What was a bustle?
a. The first padded uplifting bra
b. Lace headgear
c. Lace inserted in the bosom of a gown for modesty
d. Padding worn on a woman's bottom

89. What was a bustiere?
a. Lace to cover the bosom
b. A shawl to cover the back of the neck and cross under the bust
c. An early all-in-one undergarment
d. An early bra

90. In the 20th century, what exactly was a snood?
a. A lace veil for the back of the head
b. A small purse for carrying smelling salts and a handerchief
c. A decorative hairnet
d. White kid gloves

91. During the 1950s and 1960s, what did the term "pillbox" refer to?
a. A small hat, worn at the back of the head
b. An enamelled container for medication
c. A small handbag
d. A beret

92. During the 1960s, what items were frequently adorned with yellow polka dots?
a. Hair ribbons
b. Bra tops worn with jeans
c. Bikinis
d. Mini skirts

93. During the 1960s and 70s, what did the term "platforms" typically refer to?
a. Very high thin heels
b. The bare feet of the "hippies"
c. Highly decorated sneakers
d. Shoes with very thick soles

94. **Who gained fame as a designer for young women in the 1960s, focusing on creating short and vibrantly colored dresses?**
a. Coco Chanel
b. Twiggie
c. Jackie Kennedy
d. Mary Quant

95. **What exactly were hot pants?**
a. Very short shorts
b. Embroidered bell bottomed jeans
c. G-strings
d. Suspenders

In The Name of Fashion!

96. **True or False: Women were once expected to use a form of machinery to go swimming?**
a. True
b. False

97. **Which of the following materials was never utilized as boning in a corset?**
a. Whalebone
b. Leather
c. Wood
d. Wool

98. **What were "chopines," also known at times as "ox-muzzles"?**
a. Hats
b. Corsets
c. Footwear
d. Neck Ruffs

99. **What was a common ingredient besides vinegar used in depilatory creams popular during the 1700s?**
a. White Lead

b. Cat Faeces

c. Sour Milk

d. Ash

100. What product faced a ban attempt by the New York Board of Health in the USA in 1924?

a. Hot Wax

b. Shampoo

c. Mascara

d. Lipstick

101. Why was the early form of foundation known as "ceruse" potentially deadly during the 1300s?

a. It attracted the sun causing skin cancer

b. It never killed

c. The pores were blocked causing the wearer to suffocate

d. It was made using lead

102. In the 1700s, rather than plucking, women would shave their eyebrows and then adorn them with false ones crafted from what material?

a. Leather

b. Wool

c. Cat Fur

d. Mouse Skin

103. Which of these hazardous substances was not commonly used as a blusher during the 1700s?

a. Red Lead

b. Cyanide

c. Brimstone

d. Mercury

104. What substance, once utilized as a hair dye, was favored during ancient Egypt when glossy black hair was considered fashionable?

a. Ground Ox Hooves

b. Onion Juice

c. Cat's Wombs

d. Coal

105. Until the 1900s, Melanesian women were occasionally documented wearing what unusual item as earrings?

a. Ears
b. Elephant Tusks
c. Small Dogs
d. Birds

Watch Fashion Trivia

106. Which luxury watch brand is known for its iconic Royal Oak design?

a. Rolex
b. Patek Philippe
c. Audemars Piguet
d. Omega

107. Which material is commonly used for the construction of high-end sports watches due to its durability and lightweight properties?

a. Stainless Steel
b. Titanium
c. Gold
d. Platinum

108. The "Submariner" is a famous model line produced by which watch brand?

a. Tag Heuer
b. Breitling
c. Rolex
d. Cartier

109. **Which watch brand is famous for its partnership with the automotive industry, particularly with racing events like Formula 1?**
a. Hublot
b. TAG Heuer
c. Bell & Ross
d. Jaeger-LeCoultre

110. **Which watch complication displays the phases of the moon?**
a. Chronograph
b. Perpetual Calendar
c. Moonphase
d. Tourbillon

111. **What term describes the rotating bezel often found on diving watches used to track elapsed time underwater?**
a. Tachymeter
b. GMT
c. Dive bezel
d. Rehaut

112. **Which watch brand is famous for its association with aviation and pilot's watches?**
a. IWC Schaffhausen
b. Blancpain
c. Breguet
d. Longines

113. **The "Speedmaster" is a legendary model line produced by which watch brand?**
a. Breitling
b. Omega
c. Cartier
d. Jaeger-LeCoultre

114. **What term describes the transparent case back of a watch that allows the wearer to see the movement inside?**

a. Exhibition case back
b. Sapphire crystal
c. Skeleton dial
d. Perpetual case

115. Which watch brand is famous for its "Big Bang" collection, featuring bold and avant-garde designs?
a. Richard Mille
b. Hublot
c. Franck Muller
d. Urwerk

116. Which metal is often used to create luxury watch cases due to its lustrous appearance and resistance to corrosion?
a. Brass
b. Aluminum
c. Platinum
d. Gold

117. What term describes a watch that uses both mechanical and electronic components for timekeeping?
a. Chronometer
b. Quartz
c. Automatic
d. Hybrid

118. Which watch brand is famous for its "Nautilus" collection, known for its distinctive porthole-inspired design?
a. Audemars Piguet
b. Patek Philippe
c. Vacheron Constantin
d. Breguet

119. What is the purpose of a watch's "tachymeter" scale?
a. Measuring speed
b. Measuring distance
c. Measuring depth
d. Measuring heart rate

120. Which watch brand is famous for its "Tank" collection, inspired by the shape of military tanks?

a. Cartier
b. Chopard
c. Bulgari
d. Tiffany & Co.

ANSWERS

1. **Cleopatra**
2. **Einhard**
3. **The Adventures of Robin Hood**
4. **Yes**
5. **Pirates of the Caribbean: The Curse of the Black Pearl**
6. **The Three Musketeers**
7. **Pride and Prejudice**
8. **Johann Strauss II**
9. **Irene Castle**
10. **Star Trek: The Next Generation**
11. **Hobble skirt**
12. **Their skirts flapped up when they danced or ran**
13. **Elsa Schiaparelli**
14. **Shoulders**
15. **Poodle skirts**
16. **The Beatles**
17. **Platform shoes**
18. **Leg warmers**
19. **Grunge**

20. The unshaven look
21. Elizabeth Taylor
22. Madonna
23. Naomi Campbell
24. Bjork
25. Elizabeth Hurley
26. Michael Jackson
27. Britney Spears
28. Cher
29. Lady Gaga
30. Sacha Baron Cohen
31. Flapper Girls
32. Coco Chanel
33. Mood Rings
34. Go-Go Boots
35. Beehive
36. Miami Vice
37. Shell Suit
38. Power Dressing
39. Platforms
40. Jeans
41. Cloche
42. Stiff petticoats to 'puff out' the skirt
43. Gabrielle (Coco) Chanel
44. On the head
45. Ribbed corset
46. Qipao
47. Very pale pinks lipsticks outlined with a pencil
48. Daniel Swarovski
49. Fedora
50. Had two colours
51. acid-washed
52. buttons
53. banana clip
54. Combat boots
55. crimping
56. China Flats

57. Muscle Pants
58. Ferrari
59. Air brushed
60. Shark's Tooth
61. 1700
62. James Hargreaves - A British spinner
63. Elvis Presley
64. Christian Dior
65. Paris
66. Forms
67. Mark Eisen
68. Corsets with hoop skirts
69. Calabria, Italy
70. Props
71. By doing fashion shows
72. Jean Patou
73. 1920
74. Pret-a-porter
75. Johannesburg - South Africa
76. "Body On Tap"
77. Terrific
78. "Capezio"
79. "Dolphins"
80. Mt. Dew
81. Underoos
82. "Charlie"
83. "Kissing Potion"
84. "Satin Pants"
85. "Brut for Men"
86. A wide hoop worn under ladies' gowns
87. All of these
88. Padding worn on a woman's bottom
89. An early all-in-one undergarment
90. A decorative hairnet
91. A small hat, worn at the back of the head
92. Bikinis
93. Shoes with very thick soles

94. Mary Quant
95. Very short shorts
96. True
97. Wool
98. Footwear
99. Cat Faeces
100. Lipstick
101. It was made using lead
102. Mouse Skin
103. Cyanide
104. Cat's Wombs
105. Small Dogs
106. Audemars Piguet
107. Titanium
108. Rolex
109. TAG Heuer
110. Moonphase
111. Dive bezel
112. IWC Schaffhausen
113. Omega
114. Exhibition case back
115. Hublot
116. Gold
117. Hybrid
118. Patek Philippe
119. Measuring speed
120. Cartier

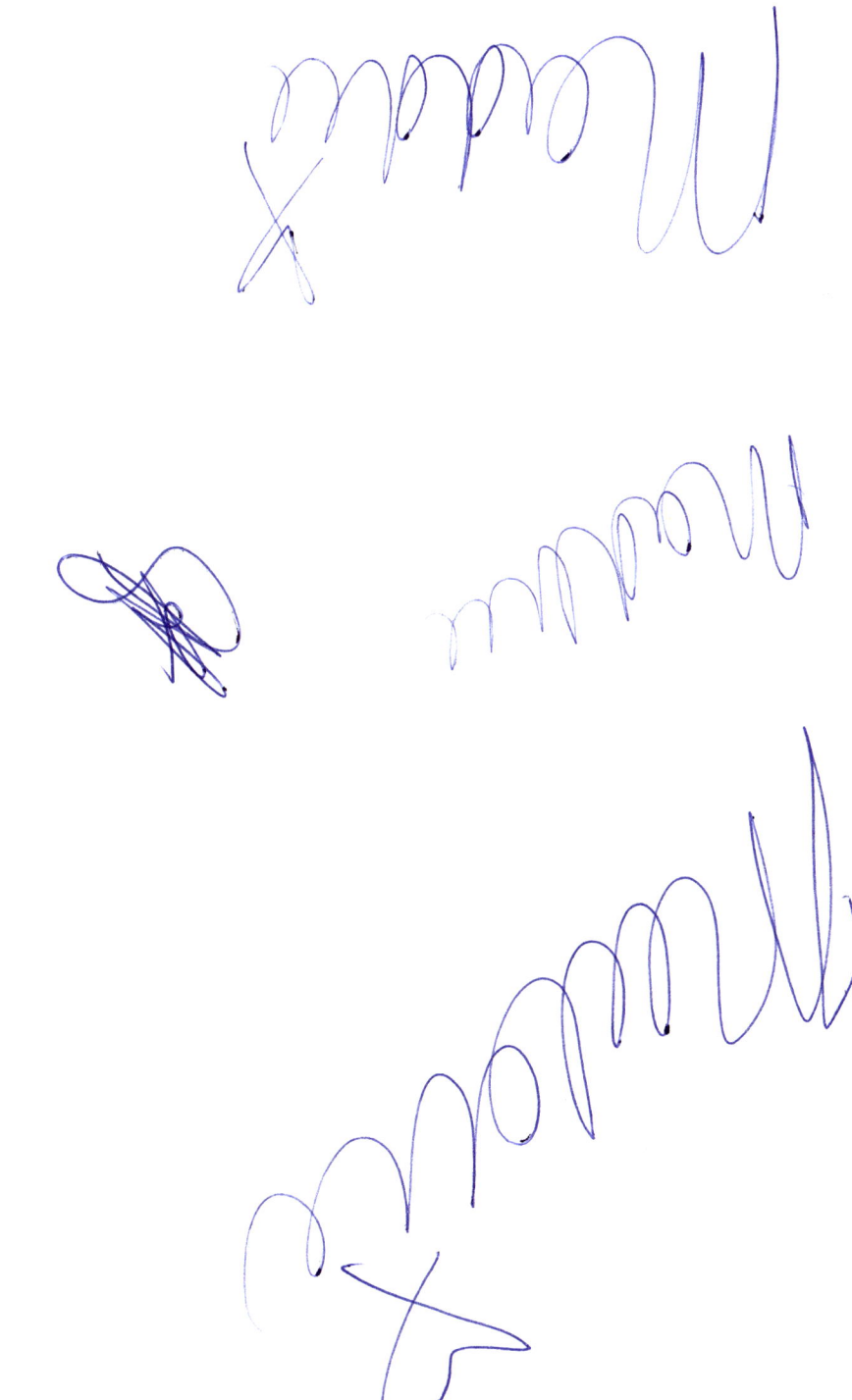

Printed in Great Britain
by Amazon

51460601R00096